WINGS OF FIRE

A COMBAT HISTORY OF THE F-15

MIKE GUARDIA

For Marie and Melanie…
And for the intrepid pilots of the F-15 Eagle and their tireless ground crews.

Also by Mike Guardia:

American Guerrilla

Shadow Commander

Hal Moore: A Soldier Once…and Always

The Fires of Babylon

Crusader

Hal Moore: A Life in Pictures

Tomcat Fury

Co-authored with Lt. General Harold G. Moore:

Hal Moore on Leadership

Contents

Introduction

The year was 1967. It was a tumultuous time for America—the Summer of Love, race riots in Detroit and Milwaukee, and a growing restlessness over the war in Vietnam. That July, at the Moscow Air Show, the Soviets unveiled six new state-of-the-art aircraft—including the MiG-23, MiG-25, and Su-11—all of which were purportedly capable of outmaneuvering any fighter jet in NATO's inventory. Meanwhile, in the skies over Vietnam, American fighter squadrons had established air superiority with the F-4 Phantom II. However, the trusted crate was rapidly growing obsolete in the face of new Soviet aircraft. Thus, in an effort to maintain parity with the dreaded Warsaw Pact, the US Air Force entered discussions for a new, lightweight, multi-role fighter. The result was the McDonnell Douglas (now Boeing) F-15 Eagle—the most successful fighter jet of the modern era.

For more than forty years, the F-15 Eagle (and its Strike Eagle variant) has been the US Air Force's premier air superiority, multi-role fighter. Made popular by its ubiquity during the Persian Gulf War, the F-15 has become one of the most recognized and revered fighter jets in the world. Introduced in 1972, the F-15 made its combat debut in the skies over Israel. American F-15s first proved their mettle during Operation Desert Storm and in the air wars over Yugoslavia. Today, the F-15 continues to serve on the frontlines in Afghanistan. Throughout its illustrious combat history, the F-15 has achieved more than one hundred air-to-air victories… *and zero losses.*

Wings of Fire is the definitive combat history of the vaunted F-15 Eagle and Strike Eagle, as told by the pilots who flew her into combat. It is to these brave pilots—and their tireless ground crews—that this book is graciously dedicated.

Design and Development

In 1943, the revised edition of Field Manual 100–20, *Command and Employment of Air Power*, outlined the critical need for air power within America's fighting forces. The opening section of the manual reads:

"The inherent flexibility of air power is its greatest asset. This flexibility makes it possible to employ the whole weight of the available air power against selected areas…such concentrated use of the air striking force is a battle-winning factor of the first importance."

From these opening remarks, it was clear that "air superiority" had become a top criterion for success on the modern battlefield. Indeed, throughout World War II, tactical and strategic air power had paved the way for numerous Allied victories on the ground.

The Mikoyan-Gurevich MiG-25 "Foxbat." A high-speed interceptor that debuted at the Moscow Air Show in 1967, the MiG-25 was purportedly capable of outmaneuvering any jet in NATO's inventory. Although much of the hype surrounding the MiG-25 subsided in later years, the McDonnell Douglas F-15 Eagle was conceived as counterbalance to the Soviet interceptor. (Dmitri Mottl)

The McDonnell Douglas F-4 Phantom II. An interceptor and fighter-bomber, the F-4 Phantom was the direct predecessor of the F-15 Eagle. Although the F-4 had achieved air superiority in the skies over Vietnam, the plane was rapidly growing obsolete in the face of newer-generation MiGs and Sukhois. (US Air Force)

Although air power could not have won the war by itself, there was little argument that the Allies' air-ground synchronization had hastened the enemy's defeat.

In Korea, UN air commanders took a slightly different approach to aerial combat than their forbearers had done during the two World Wars. Air superiority was still the overarching goal—but their methods and equipment had changed. For the first time in history, American pilots had harnessed the power of jet aircraft. Mounted aboard the new F-86 Sabre, Air Force pilots took to the sky in combat against the MiG-15. During these dogfights, American pilots devastated the enemy with a kill/loss ratio of nearly 10 to 1. Indeed, by the fall of 1950, the North Koreans had lost 110 of their 132 aircraft.

Following the war in Korea, however, President Dwight D. Eisenhower shifted America's defense posture to one of nuclear deterrence. Unwittingly or not, these new defense policies disrupted the long-standing notions of air power. At the time, America's premiere fighter aircraft was the F-100 series—designed to locate and destroy nuclear targets rather than engage in aerial combat. Thus, a new generation of tactical aircraft had exchanged maneuverability for penetration—turning a generation of fighter pilots into little more than ground-attack aviators.

By the start of America's combat mission in Vietnam, the downstream effects of this "nuclear deterrent" policy had become apparent. During the Korean war, American pilots had boasted a 10 to 1 kill/loss ratio; in the opening days of Vietnam, however, that ratio had fallen to *3 to 1*. After years of conducting alert-status drills and stationary target practice, American fighter pilots had lost much of their dogfighting skills. As General

The first F-15A prototype on its historic first flight – July 27, 1972 at Edwards Air Force Base, California. (US Air Force)

Bruce Holloway, the Air Force Vice-Chief of Staff, famously quipped: "The tactical fighter became less and less an air superiority system and more and more what was once called an attack aircraft." For the US Air Force, the issue was clear: Something had to be done to regain the lost art of air combat maneuvering; something had to be done to reconcile the need for aerial combat against the need for long-range strike capabilities of the Nuclear Era.

But even before these exigencies had become apparent, the Navy and Air Force had been clamoring for a new fighter jet. Come what may, US naval and air commanders were certain that their existing fleets of F-4 Phantoms, A-4 Skyhawks, and F-8 Crusaders couldn't keep pace with the current and forthcoming generation of Soviet MiGs. Although the Navy and Air Force had different operational requirements—and thus needed different aircraft—both services were nevertheless ordered to find a common design that could satisfy their collective needs.

From these demands grew the Tactical Fighter Experimental (TFX) program. Under the auspices of Defense Secretary Robert McNamara, TFX debuted in 1961 and, in many ways, applied the same "bean-counter," metrics-based leadership that had won him accolades during his tenure with the Ford Motor Company. Accordingly, McNamara hypothecated that the Navy and Air Force could use a common airframe—giving the former its much-needed carrier interceptor, while giving the latter an agile, supersonic fighter jet capable of outmaneuvering enemy MiGs and surface-to-air missiles. It was a laudable idea (and not completely unprecedented, as the two services were currently sharing the F-4 Phantom II), but to fulfill their operational needs in the face of the ever-evolving Soviet menace, the US Navy and Air Force needed to "start from scratch" and

The cockpit and instrument panel of the F-15A Eagle, as seen at Holloman Air Force Base in 1980. (US Air Force)

An F-15A Eagle from the 9th Tactical Fighter Squadron prepares for flight at RAF Alconbury, 1980. (US Air Force)

design their own respective fighter jets.

When TFX launched in the spring of 1961, it may have accomplished its goal to create a common airframe. From the outset, however, the design and work-flow processes were marred by "bad blood" and other inter-service politics. For instance, McNamara had named Secretary of the Air Force, Eugene Zuckert, to be the head of TFX—a move that angered Navy Secretary John Connally, who had earlier requested to be the program's director. Although McNamara had instructed the Air Force to work closely with the Navy, organizational politics between the two services had already laid the foundations for inefficiency.

Nevertheless, TFX initiated the design phase by soliciting proposals from three leading aircraft manufacturers—Grumman, Boeing, and General Dynamics. Throughout the design process, Air Force and Navy planners rarely agreed. Most designs failed to meet the Navy's carrier requirements, necessitating numerous redesigns and tediously adding more time to the process. Finally, after months of review and redesigns, General Dynamics won the bid. Officially labeled the "F-111," General Dynamics moved swiftly into the prototype phase, but neither the Navy nor the Air Force were completely satisfied with the end product. In fact, by 1963, the F-111 had garnered such negative publicity that Congress launched an investigation into the TFX program. This put both McNamara and President Kennedy on the defensive, as both men were forced to justify the enormous spending for a fighter jet whose performance seemed marginal at best. In fact, during a 1963 news conference, President Kennedy stated:

> "My judgment is that the decision reached by Secretary McNamara was the right one, sound one, and any fair and objective hearing will bring that out. Mr. McNamara chose the plane he chose because he felt it most efficient, because he thought it would do the job and because he thought it would save the Government hundreds of millions of dollars."

In the shrouds of Neuschwanstein Castle, three American F-15s follow a West German F-104 Starfighter during an annual training exercise, 1982. (US Air Force)

Perhaps serendipitously, the investigation found nothing actionable regarding the F-111. The plane was subsequently delivered to the US Air Force in October 1964. Secretary McNamara, meanwhile, declared that the fighter jet was "the greatest single step forward in combat aircraft in several decades."

In hindsight, however, historians agree that the F-111 was ill-suited for air-to-air combat. Military test pilot George Marrett, for example, admitted that the F-111 was "grossly underpowered, and had poor cockpit visibility for a fighter." The F-111 did, however, perform well as a ground-attack aircraft—a role which the plane regularly fulfilled until the end of its service life. The F-111 also excelled as a long-range interceptor and as an electronic warfare asset. "I wouldn't want to maneuver one against a fighter," Marrett continued, "but purely as an interceptor, it would have done well against bombers and cruise missiles." Eventually, even McNamara conceded that the F-111 had been a poor choice for the TFX program. Despite the F-111's "saving grace" as a latter-day attack aircraft, the Air Force still needed a new fighter jet.

Returning to the proverbial "drawing board," the Air Force re-examined its minimum requirements for the experimental fighter. First, they needed a jet with a Short Takeoff and Landing (STOL) capability. Accordingly, the fighter would have to clear a 50-foot obstacle on a 3,000-foot runway, with a minimum takeoff weight of 4,000 pounds. Second, the jet would need a 230-nautical mile radius on internal fuel, with a 2,600-nautical mile ferry range from an external fuel source. Third, the plane needed to be fast—with a top speed of at least Mach 2. Finally, the Air Force wanted its jet to have a one-man crew; they did not foresee the need for a two-person cockpit, as the Navy had done for the F-14.

Meanwhile, General Arthur Agan, commander of the Air Force's Aerospace Defense Command, took note of the ailing TFX program and the calamitous debut of the F-111. A distinguished P-38 pilot who had flown more than 200 combat missions over the European theater, Agan understood the need for a smaller and more agile fighter jet. Moreover, Agan believed that high-performance aircraft could survive the first volleys of a nuclear war and continue facilitating the destruction of enemy forces. His plan was thus to ensure that the Air Force acquired such a plane for its air superiority missions. According to General Agan, the current fleet of F-111s and F-4s were now obsolete, and the Air Force's inventory "must contain other aircraft." Although Agan admitted that his contemporaries had different ideas for how America's next fighter jet should operate, he hoped that extensive aerial testing and wargaming could facilitate a consensus. "My own belief," he continued, "is that a smaller aircraft than the F-111, and possibly than the F-4, is needed – and needed now. It can be smaller because we can plan to use it for air superiority and close air support. We can accept less range because the majority of the targets which we expect in close air support will be within 250 miles (400 km) of the forward edge of the battle area. We can accept less payload because of the improved ordnance and more accurate delivery of weapons. Such an aircraft may be able to win the air superiority fight over the battlefield. It should be a medium-cost aircraft, because we will need many."

General Agan understood the complexity of the F-111 program, and Secretary McNamara's personal attachment to it. Thus, instead of condemning the F-111 outright, Agan chose a different tact—he would assemble a coterie of distinguished fighter pilots in an effort to convince McNamara of the need to develop a *new* fighter jet. Agan and his crew recognized that the Soviets' fighter aircraft had leapt a generation ahead of their US counterparts. Of particular concern was the MiG-21 "Fishbed," introduced

An F-15 leads two West German Tornado jets on aerial maneuvers in Europe, 1982. (US Air Force)

in 1956 and boasting a range of 400 nautical miles. To make matters worse, the MiG-23 and MiG-25 were on the horizon. To carry on with the obsolete F-4 and F-100 series, Agan argued, would undermine America's air superiority and jeopardize national security. Agan's group also concluded that most aerial engagements occurred at speeds up to Mach 1.6 and at altitudes up to 30,000 feet. At present, there wasn't a single fighter in the US inventory that could perform to those specifications…and air-to-air missiles wouldn't solve the problem.

The need for a close-combat fighter became more apparent as the air war in Vietnam raged into its sophomore year. Indeed, the US was losing the pride of its aerial fleet to Communist aircraft heretofore considered inferior. For instance, two American F-105s were shot down by obsolete MiGs during a bombing run over Vietnam. To make matter worse, the entire fleet of B-26 Invaders in Vietnam had been grounded following the in-flight loss of a wing during a practice strafing run at Eglin Air Force Base. Aghast, the Pentagon realized it could no longer remain complacent about the aging status of its fighter and tactical aircraft. With a slightly renewed vigor, Robert McNamara authorized $10 million for the development of a new fighter aircraft—nimble enough for air-to-air combat, yet durable enough for ground attack operations. The new program was now labeled the Fighter Experimental (F-X).

The Air Force wanted its new aircraft to be lithe and lean, with a radar capability similar to the F-4 Phantom. More importantly, however, the F-X had to be operational by 1970. The Director of Operational Requirements and Development Plans (DOR&DP) also advised that the F-X be built around the capabilities for close air support, armed reconnaissance, and night/day surveillance. Tactical Air Command (TAC), meanwhile, stressed maneuverability and a high thrust-to-weight ratio.

On December 8, 1965, the Air Force sent proposal requests to thirteen aircraft manufacturers. Of the initial thirteen contacted, four replied—including Boeing, Lockheed, North American, and Grumman. Each of their designs, however, fell short of what Air Force had anticipated. According to their own specifications, the Air Force wanted a fighter that could accommodate the latest avionics, provide a substantial payload capacity, while offering great maneuverability at increased speeds with a higher operational radius. The final product, however, was projected to weigh more than 60,000 pounds. Taken together, the cost and weight considerations had rendered the plane unusable as a fighter jet.

While contemplating how to improve their beleaguered F-X program, the Air Force took warning of the latest Soviet interceptor—the MiG-25 (NATO Reporting Name: "Foxbat"). Although the MiG-25 had not yet been proven in combat, the jet was breaking airspeed records for East and West. In March 1965, for example, the jet flew more than 1,440 miles per hour on a 1,000-kilometer circuit. During the same flight trial, it climbed to more than 65,000 feet in under three minutes. Later that year, the MiG-25 also set a new world altitude record for payload and non-payload flights.

These were numbers the likes of which the West had never seen.

Indeed, the MiG-25 could fly at speeds in excess of Mach 3 and reach altitudes heretofore deemed unreachable for a tactical fighter. The greater problem for the US Air

American F-15s intercept Soviet Tu-95 reconnaissance planes along the frontiers of American airspace, a recurring episode during the latter decades of the Cold War. Most of these interceptions passed without incident, with the Tu-95s being escorted back to an acceptable distance. (US Air Force)

Force, however, was that they had no idea how the Soviets had cobbled together such a "masterpiece" of modern engineering. By the same token, however, the appearance of the MiG-25 motivated the F-X planners to work harder. To counter the ever-evolving threat from Soviet aircraft, the Air Force needed something of equal or greater value.

Existing intelligence on the MiG-25, however, was based on little more than second-hand information. Western analysts knew, for example, that the plane was fast—but the only public photos they had seen of the Foxbat were from the Moscow Air Show in July 1967. Four years later, during the Arab-Israeli "War of Attrition," an Israeli F-4 Phantom tried to intercept a Soviet MiG-25 flying reconnaissance for the Egyptians. The engagement was short-lived, however, as the MiG pilot thrust his engines to full afterburner, leaving the F-4 Phantom behind at a speed of Mach 3.2.

Stories like this fueled the development of the F-15 Eagle. The recurring problem, however, was that the Air Force had so little information on the Soviet interceptor. Other than the Foxbat's reported speed, the US knew virtually nothing of the MiG-

An F–15C from the 1st Tactical Fighter Wing stands silhouetted against the morning sun during Exercise Gallant Eagle '86 at Davis-Monthan Air Force Base, Arizona. (US Air Force)

25's capabilities. Thus, the F-X developers had to make several assumptions. They had to assume that the MiG-25 could do everything that an ideal multi-role fighter could do: fly fast at any angle, fly long distances, and be nimble enough for air-to-air combat. American military analysts also assumed that the Foxbat was powered by turbofan engines and that its body was constructed from a lightweight, composite material. The Air Force then pondered how to modify the F-X to match these assumptions.

Ironically, the US would later discover many of their assumptions regarding the MiG-25 were wrong. In September 1976, Lieutenant Viktor Belenko, a Soviet fighter pilot, defected and flew his MiG-25 to Japan, bringing with him the highly-classified Pilot's Manual. Taking custody of both Belenko and his plane, the US had its first chance to deconstruct the legendary MiG-25. The reality, however, was that this so-called "interceptor" was a poorly-engineered death trap with an oversized motor.

American scientists and engineers quickly discovered that the MiG-25 was never designed for close combat, and the plane was difficult to maneuver. Indeed, its sole purpose was to fly fast. The airframe's construction was rather simple and the craftsmanship was shoddy. To boot, the plane was much heavier than expected, its fuel economy was lower than expected, and it was hardly maneuverable at lower speeds. In fact, the MiG-25 prototypes that had broken airspeed records a decade earlier had been made from different materials—just for breaking those records. Indeed, those prototypes could never have functioned in aerial combat.

Although the MiG-25 (and many of its latter-day stablemates) proved to be a disappointment, its appearance nonetheless motivated the US Air Force to create an unparalleled fighter. To this end, they enlisted the help of Major John R. Boyd—a distinguished fighter pilot and one of the leading experts on modern warfare. Among his many contributions to the field of military science, Boyd had devised a concept known as Energy Maneuverability (EM), during his time as an engineering graduate student at

Three F-15A Eagles from the 199th Fighter Squadron, Hawaii Air National Guard, fire their AIM-7 Sparrow missiles in unison over Hickam Air Force Base. (US Air Force)

Georgia Tech. Boyd's EM theory was a way of calculating and discussing the way energy changes for a jet during flight and measuring its maneuverability potential. The EM principles could determine what was possible for altitude changes, airspeed limits, and adjustments in direction. It was, by most accounts, "a revolutionary analytical technique that permitted 'fighter' jocks to communicate with engineers. The EM theory expressed in numbers what fighter pilots had been trying to say for years by moving their hands. It also permitted planners and developers to compare competing aircraft directly and to demonstrate the effects of design changes on aircraft performance."

Boyd joined the F-X program in October 1966. By the spring of 1967, his EM theory had helped the Air Force create a preliminary design for a jet that was that 40,000 pounds, with a thrust to weight ratio of .97, and a top speed of Mach 2.5. With these technical specifications in mind, the Air Force continued making adjustments to the prototype design, creating a finalized cost estimate and a developmental timeline. In the final proposal, the cost came to $2.84 million per jet; $615 million for research and development; $4.1 billion for procurement; and nearly $2.5 billion for operations and maintenance for an estimated 1,000 aircraft.

Throughout the design phase for the F-15, one persistent roadblock was the notion that the Navy and Air Force had to share a common plane—much as they had done with the F-4 Phantom in Vietnam. By 1968, however, it was clear that both services had their own special needs and requirements. Thus, both services needed their own uniquely-designed airplanes. To boot, neither service wanted to continue playing the game of aircraft "commonality" with the skinflint politicians on Capitol Hill. Thus, the Air Force

An American F-15C Eagle from the 22nd Tactical Fighter Squadron over Bitburg Air Base in West Germany, April 1988. (US Air Force)

abandoned the political game, stating that they wanted something agile, maneuverable, and exclusively for air-to-air combat. Indeed, the Air Force wanted its new fighter to do one thing: *establish air superiority*. There would be *no* ground-attack considerations made when designing the airframe. In fact, during a testimony to the Senate Armed Services Committee in May 1968, General McConnell stated:

> "We had a very difficult time in satisfying all the people who had to be satisfied as to what the F-X was going to be. In fact, we had a difficult time within the Air Force. There were a lot of people in the Air Force who wanted to make the F-X into another F-4 type of aircraft. We finally decided—and I hope there is no one who still disagrees—that this aircraft is going to be an air superiority fighter."

Humorously, when one senator pressed whether the F-X would be used for close air support, McConnell replied: "It would be over my dead body."

By the fall of 1968, the Air Force had approved the final design and was ready to enter the developmental contract phase. According to their Development Concept Paper, the Air Force outlined four critical parameters for the experimental F-15:

1. A 260 nautical mile mission radius

2. 60-nm terminal dash with between 2.5 and 3 minutes of max-power combat time

3. Sea level max speed of Mach 1.2

4. Max speed of 2.3, with burst capability of Mach 2.5

On September 30, 1968, the Air Force once again solicited bids from America's leading aircraft companies. Four of them responded—including General Dynamics, Northrop, McDonnell Douglas, and Fairchild-Hiller. Each of the aerospace firms were asked to submit their proposals by the following June, to include cost estimates and production timelines. Reviewing the bids, Air Force leaders evaluated each design against a pre-determined list of 87 design factors. This allowed the evaluation process to remain impartial and facilitate selection based on an aggregate score of the listed factors - along with the comparative cost and timeline from each company. After several months of review, the Air Force ultimately awarded the contract to McDonnell Douglas on December 15, 1969.

It was a great win for the St. Louis-based aircraft manufacturer, having spent two years on the project and investing more than two million man-hours into the concept and contract portions alone. Moreover, this winning bid saved nearly 10,000 jobs at McDonnell Douglas, many of which were holdovers from the F-4 Phantom II program.

With a manufacturer selected—and with new doctrines of air superiority under review— excitement rang high within the fighter jock community. In fact, Brigadier General Benjamin N. Bellis, the inaugural director of the F-15 program, cheerfully predicted that:

> "We will not only produce the #1 aircraft in the US inventory, but also reestablish the Air Force's credibility as a manager of major weapon system programs and regain the confidence and support of the Congress and the taxpayer."

But McDonnell Douglas now faced the monumental task of building a plane that

Two F-15A Eagles from the 199th Fighter Squadron in formation over Honolulu, Hawaii in 1988. (US Air Force)

A prototype F-15E Strike Eagle, circa 1987. Although the F-15 had originally been conceived as a pure air-superiority fighter with "not one pound for air-to-ground," the US Air Force later contracted McDonnell Douglas to develop a ground-attack variant. The result was the F-15E, which fulfilled the role of a true "strike fighter," a plane that could simultaneously be an air superiority fighter and an attack aircraft. (US Air Force)

could meet the Air Force's expectations.

Fortunately, McDonnell Douglas wouldn't be alone. Indeed, as the scientists and engineers began refining their ideas for the jet's maneuverability, the aerospace giant began outsourcing development of the F-15's subsystems to third-party contractors. The engine, for example, would be a Pratt & Whitney design—an augmented twin-spool, axial-flow gas turbine. Weighing approximately 2,800 pounds, the Pratt & Whitney engine created more than 22,000 pounds of thrust. Pratt & Whitney ultimately won the contract after demonstrating that they could build a common core for *two* separate engines—one for the F-15; another for the Navy's F-14. The F-15 would carry the Pratt & Whitney F100-PW-100 engine, while the Navy ultimately selected the smaller Pratt & Whitney TF40 for its first-generation F-14s. Aboard the F-14, however, this TF40 was terribly underpowered for the airframe, and frequently malfunctioned in flight. In fact, for the F-14A, nearly 28 percent of all accidents were caused by engine failure. Aboard the F-15, however, the F100 engine was delivered on time and passed the milestones needed for its inaugural flight.

For the on-board radar, McDonnell Douglas evaluated two firms: Westinghouse Electric and Hughes Aircraft. Because the first-generation F-15 would not have a co-pilot or radar intercept officer, the radar design had to be usable by the pilot alone. This radar also had to be multi-functional for long-range intercepts and air combat maneuvering. After testing both designs in more than one hundred flights, McDonnell Douglas awarded the radar contract to Hughes Aircraft.

For the onboard weapon systems, the F-15 would use existing missile technology. However, the war in Vietnam had inspired the Air Force to fit the plane with an improved aero-cannon. General Electric and Ford-Philco submitted designs, with the latter featuring a caseless ammunition platform. Ford-Philco's design, however, suffered numerous developmental problems and was dropped in favor of General Electric's M61 Vulcan gun.

With the pieces in place and the players aligned, the F-15 drew nearer to its maiden flight. Still, the Air Force felt pressured to deliver its new fighter ahead of schedule. The Navy was concurrently developing the F-14 and, in the spirit of interservice rivalry, the Air Force did not want to be outdone in the bid for priority defense dollars. Inter-agency competitions aside, however, the greater sense of urgency was the need to counter the MiG-25. Real or perceived, these threats from the latest-generation Soviet interceptors was such that the Pentagon could not ignore. To this end, the Air Force solicited help from NASA. With America's space agency at the helm, the F-15 underwent a series of tests that identified the plane's weaknesses and highlighted areas for improvement. One example was a heretofore unidentified problem with the F-15's tailfin. Indeed, NASA's engineers had discovered that the F-15's subsonic drag was too high—prompting removal of the ventral fins and an enlargement of the vertical stabilizers. General Bellis described the process in a 1971 testimony to the Senate Armed Forces Committee:

> "The radome [an on-board enclosure protecting the aircraft's radar] has been made more symmetrical to enhance the radar performance. Cowl fences have been added to the upper outer edge of the inlet to improve directional stability. The inlets have been refined. The bluntness of the cowl lip has been changed. The wing and horizontal tail were both moved 5 inches...to improve aircraft balance and maintain the desired handling qualities and stability. To improve the external aerodynamics, the aft section of the aircraft has undergone some refinement; this includes modified lines, ventral removal, and increased vertical tail height."

The F-15E Strike Eagle in flight. Unlike its air superiority cousin, the F-15E is a standard two-seat aircraft, accommodating the pilot and the back-seat Weapon Systems Officer (WSO), who aids in weapons employment, surveillance, target acquisition, and navigation. (US Air Force)

Development and production continued into 1972, whereupon the F-15 was officially branded the "Eagle." And on June 26, 1972, the F-15 Eagle made its public debut at the McDonnell Douglas plant in St. Louis.

The following day, the plane made its inaugural flight.

Piloted by Irving L. Burrows—McDonnel Douglas's Chief Experimental Test Pilot— the F-15 Eagle flew its maiden voyage from Edwards Air Force Base in California. During the fifty-minute flight, the Eagle reached an altitude of 12,000 feet and a top speed of 320 mph. While the jet was certainly capable of higher speeds at higher altitudes, this maiden flight was only intended to test the Eagle's airworthiness and overall handling. Test flights continued over the next several months, and by November 1972, the jet had reached heights in excess of 60,000 feet and speeds in excess of Mach 2.3.

As these test flights continued, the Air Force maintained its working relationship with NASA - cycling the F-15 through various wind tunnel evaluations, structural tests, and flight simulations. Indeed, every angle, curve, and system aboard the F-15 was tested before moving the plane into full-scale production. Once completed, however, the F-15 Eagle was ready to become the air superiority jet fighter that had many had envisioned.

From its conception during Vietnam, to its development within the workshops of McDonnell Douglas, the F-15 Eagle had a long journey. But its long and tedious production had been well worth the wait.

In January 1976, the first fully-operational F-15 Eagle arrived at the 555th Tactical Fighter Squadron at Luke Air Force Base, Arizona. Over the next several decades, five sequentially-lettered variants of the F-15 were delivered to US Air Force squadrons

Three F-15E Strike Eagles stand in silhouette on the tarmac. (US Air Force)

worldwide. The F-15A was the first operational variant designated for squadron use. Between 1972-79, nearly 400 A-variants were built. The F-15A's contemporary variant, the F-15B, was a two-seat trainer relegated to the Air Force's flight school units. The F-15C, produced between 1979-1985, featured the same airframe and single-seat cockpit of the A-variant, but with improved avionics—including the AN/APG-70 radar. The parallel-produced F-15D was also a two-seat trainer, but made to accommodate the upgrades of the C-variant.

Perhaps the most prominent of the Eagle variants, however, was the F-15E Strike Eagle. A standard two-seat, all-weather, multi-role strike fighter, the F-15E doubles as both an air superiority fighter *and* an attack aircraft. Developed in the 1980s, the F-15E was built for high-speed, long-range air interdictions without the need for additional support aircraft. The Strike Eagles are generally distinguishable from the base-model F-15s by the latter's two-seat tandem cockpit, additional fuel tanks, and darker camouflage schemes. Aside from these modifications, the Strike Eagle uses the same basic airframe and differs little from the earlier F-15 variants.

Because the first-generation F-15 was designed exclusively for air superiority, the Air Force continued to rely on the F-4 Phantom and F-111 to fulfill the ground-attack role. In fact, the opposition to incorporating ground attack capabilities into the original F-15 was so fierce that the program managers had been chanting: "Not one pound for air to ground."

Despite the Pentagon's lack of interest, McDonnell Douglas began working quietly on an F-15 variant to fulfill the role of a "strike fighter"—a plane that could presumably perform air superiority and ground-attack missions. Ultimately, McDonnell Douglas envisioned an aircraft that could replace both the F-111 and F-4, and augment the existing fleet of base-model F-15s. After submitting their proposals to the Air Force's Tactical All-Weather Requirement Study in 1978, McDonnell Douglas emerged as the winner to provide the next-generation strike fighter. The following year, McDonnell Douglas partnered with Hughes Aircraft to begin development of the F-15E and its air-to-ground capabilities.

An F-15E Strike Eagle from the 333d Fighter Squadron patrols the airspace surrounding the Space Shuttle Atlantis as it launches onto its final voyage—May 2010. (US Air Force)

To facilitate the F-15E's production, McDonnell Douglas modified an existing F-15B as a demonstrator. Officially termed the "Advanced Fighter Capability Demonstrator," the experimental aircraft took its maiden flight on July 8, 1980. Aside from displaying its additional, conformal fuel tanks, this F-15E demonstrator was also fitted with a Pave Tack laser-designator targeting pod to facilitate the delivery of guided munitions.

Not coincidentally, in March 1981, the Air Force launched the Enhanced Tactical Fighter program to find a replacement for the F-111. Later renamed the Dual-Role

Fighter (DRF) program, the competition drew entries from General Dynamics, McDonnell Douglas, and the West German aerospace giant Panavia Aircraft. DRF envisioned an aircraft capable of both air superiority missions and multi-faceted air interdictions. General Dynamics submitted the F–16XL; McDonnell-Douglas submitted the F–15E; while Panavia submitted its much-vaunted Tornado.

Under the leadership of Brigadier General Ronald W. Yates, DRF evaluated the three contenders for nearly two years. During these extensive trials, the F–15E logged more than 200 flights under various mission parameters. The F–16 variant likewise performed well, but the Air Force ultimately chose the F–15E due to its lower developmental costs. The Tornado, by contrast, was screened out of the competition early, as the evaluators were not particularly impressed by its performance.

Series production of the F–15E began in July 1985—the first of which made its maiden flight on December 11, 1986. Piloted by McDonnell Douglas test pilot Gary Jennings, the inaugural F–15E reached an airspeed of Mach 0.9 and an altitude of 40,000 feet during its 75-minute flight. The first fully-operational F–15E arrived at the 405th Tactical Training Wing at Luke Air Force Base, Arizona, in April 1988. Unlike its predecessors, the F–15E's production continued well into the 2000s. As of 2019, more than 230 Strike Eagles have been fielded to the US Air Force, and the Strike Eagle variant is expected to remain in service beyond the year 2025.

The Fires of Galilee

Emerging victorious from the Yom Kippur War of 1973, the Israeli Defense Forces (IDF) took a critical look at their tactical air squadrons. With the Mirage III and F-4 Phantom II, the Israelis had established air superiority in the Middle East but could not maintain that position with their current fleet of rapidly-aging fighters. Meanwhile, Iraq, Egypt, Syria—stung by their latest defeat at the hands of the IDF—solicited the Soviet Union for the newest generation of MiG aircraft. Thus, to defend the skies over Judea, the Israeli Air Force would have to upgrade their tactical air fleets.

In the wake of the Six Day War, Israeli air commanders had approached the US government, soliciting the F-4 Phantom II as a safeguard against Arab aggression. Taking note of its combat performance in Vietnam, IDF leaders thought the F-4 Phantom would give them the technological edge they needed to maintain air superiority over the Mediterranean—especially in the face of Arab MiG-21s and MiG-23s. Israel received a handful of F-4 Phantoms in the fall of 1969, during their so-called "War of Attrition"—a bloody three-year conflict involving Egypt, Jordan, and the Palestinian Liberation Organization (PLO). In November 1969, IDF pilot Sam Hertz achieved the first aerial victory for an Israeli F-4—skillfully downing a MiG-21 with an air-to-air missile. Throughout the War of Attrition, Israeli F-4s compiled 116 air combat victories with a kill-loss ratio of 25 to 1.

But as the F-4 proved its mettle in combat against Arab MiGs and Sukhois, the trusty crate was becoming obsolete. With the advent of new avionics, onboard targeting computers, and "fly-by-wire" systems, a new generation of fighter aircraft had emerged. Indeed, by 1979, many Arab air forces had received the MiG-25 and Sukhoi Su-22—both of which were purportedly hallmarks of the Digital Era. As aviation technology evolved, however, so too did the tactics of aerial combat. Seeing their Arab enemies reap the benefits of these tactical and technological changes, IDF leaders knew that they had to do likewise.

The Israeli Air Force had expressed interest in the F-15 since the end of the Yom Kippur War in 1973. The war had lasted a mere nineteen days, but the conflict had taken a heavy toll on the Israeli Air Force—103 aircraft lost with an additional 200 planes severely

An Israeli F-15 "Baz" at Tel Nof Air Base. Following the Yom Kippur War in 1973, the Israeli Air Force solicited the US government for a new fighter jet. Israeli flyers test-piloted the F-14 Tomcat and F-15 Eagle in a series of mock engagements. Ultimately, the Israeli Air Force selected the F-15 as replacement for their F-4 Phantoms. The F-15 Eagle achieved its first air-to-air victory in Israeli service, downing a Syrian MiG-21 in 1979. (Zachi Evenor)

damaged. Although the Israelis had fared better than their opponents, these losses represented nearly *twenty-five percent* of the IDF's tactical air fleet.

Israel was determined to never again suffer losses of that magnitude.

In the summer of 1974, IDF leaders made their initial bid for the newly-minted F-15 Eagle. Although the US did not immediately agree to sell the aircraft, the Pentagon nevertheless invited the Israelis to test-pilot the F-15 Eagle *and* F-14 Tomcat in a series of trials conducted at stateside air bases. The Israeli Air Force accepted the offer, and the selected pilots were eager to find a replacement for their aging and battered F-4 squadrons.

Thus, in 1974, Israeli pilot Benjamin "Beni" Peled became the first non-American to fly the F-15. Taking off from Edwards Air Force Base in California, Peled was impressed by the cockpit design and the plane's overall handling. However, he couldn't determine the F-15's combat potential since the aircraft was, after all, still in its experimental phase. Meanwhile, Israeli pilot David Ivry flew the F-14 at Naval Air Station Miramar in a variety of training scenarios against the A-4 Skyhawk. Ivry was mildly impressed by the Tomcat but found its controls "clumsy."

Almost simultaneously, Israeli Air Force pilot Amnon Arad gathered a team of seasoned fighter pilots for the next round of evaluations. Arad was a highly decorated F-4 pilot and was eager to see how the F-14 and F-15 would measure against the IDF's legacy aircraft. Rounding out his team of pilots were Assaf Ben-Nun, Omri Afek, and Israel Bahrav—all of whom were distinguished fighter pilots. Together, the Israeli pilots devised a battery of training missions to assess the aircrafts' performance. These missions would separately evaluate the F-14 and F-15 in their ability to intercept enemy aircraft and perform escort missions.

Two Israeli F-15s conduct a commemorative fly-over at the Auschwitz extermination camp in Poland. (IDF)

Arad and his fellow pilots enjoyed the evaluation process but wanted to see the F–14 and F–15 fly against one another in a simulated dogfight. After all, they reasoned, what better way to evaluate the two fighters than to pit them against one another in a combat scenario? Although impressed by the Israelis' enthusiasm, the US denied their request for an Eagle-Tomcat matchup, selecting instead the F-4 Phantom and A-4 Skyhawk as their mock aggressors.

Over the next few months, Israeli pilots completed nine test flights aboard the F-15 Eagle and F-14 Tomcat.

In the end, the Israelis preferred the F-15.

They were impressed by the plane's on-board avionics and felt that its cockpit gave them a greater perspective of the aerial battlespace. To boot, the F-15's airspeed, maneuverability, and thrust-to-weight ratio outmatched any plane in the Arab arsenal. The only drawback was the airframe's size. With a tare weight of 28,000 pounds and a wingspan of nearly 43 feet, the F-15 was larger than any fighter jet the Israelis had ever flown. Most Israeli pilots preferred a smaller girth for aerial combat.

Although impressed by the Tomcat, Israeli pilots felt that the F-14 fell short in three critical areas. First, they were dissatisfied with the canopy shape. Aboard the F-14, the canopy was framed and more in-line with the fuselage. On the F-15, however, the canopy was bubble-shaped, giving the pilot more visibility. Second, the thrust-to-weight ratio for the F-14 was smaller than the F-15. Third, the Israelis did not find the F-14's avionics to be "user-friendly."

Additionally, the F-14's energy state dropped precipitously during Within-Visual-Range (WVR) combat scenarios, giving her no edge over the A-4 Skyhawk aggressor that she was expected to outperform. The Tomcat also carried a significantly higher price tag and its anticipated maintenance costs were considerably higher than the F-15's.

However, the Israelis' assessment of the F-14 did not necessarily mean that the Tomcat was an inferior aircraft. Indeed, the F-14 Tomcat and F-15 Eagle were designed to accommodate different battlefronts. The F-14 was a two-seat, multirole aircraft designed to protect American carrier groups at sea. The F-15, on the other hand, was a single-seat fighter designed for air superiority across multiple environments. Both, however, were capable of flying long distances and fighting from beyond visual range. And although the Israeli Air Force rejected the F-14, the Shah of Iran took a keen interest in the Tomcat. Impressed by its maneuverability and multirole functionality, the Imperial Iranian Air Force selected the F-14 as its primary fighter. Today, Iran is the last remaining operator of the F-14 Tomcat.

Satisfied by the F-15's performance, the Israeli Air Force intended to purchase more than 100 F-15 variants from McDonnell Douglas between 1976 and 1999. However, amidst economic failures, diplomatic disappointments, and political pressure from Egypt, the Israelis amended their purchase agreement—receiving only *twenty-five* F-15s by the end of the 1970s. Nevertheless, this amended agreement set the stage for the IDF to maintain its air superiority over the Middle East.

To familiarize Israeli pilots with their new crate, the US created an introductory course at Randolph Air Force Base in San Antonio, Texas. Shortly thereafter, Israeli pilots flew their first solos aboard the F-15 in September 1976. The Israeli Air Force nicknamed their new crate "Baz" (Hebrew for *falcon*) and would dub their inaugural fighter unit the "Double Tail Squadron"—officially activated in November 1976 at Tel Nof Air Base in Rehovost, Israel.

On the heels of that squadron's activation, however, Israel and Egypt submitted to further negotiations, this time under the helm of President Jimmy Carter. All seemed poised for a lasting peace between Israel and her Arab neighbors, but the PLO had other ideas.

Taking advantage of the chaos amidst the Lebanese Civil War, the PLO established a base of operations in southern Lebanon. Confident in the safety of their cross-border sanctuaries, the PLO began launching raids into northern Israel. On March 11, 1978, eleven members of the PLO faction, *Fatah*, infiltrated the Israeli town of Ma'agan Michael, a waterfront community near Haifa. After firing their weapons into oncoming traffic along the coastal highway, PLO operatives hijacked a passenger bus—leading to a shootout with the local Israeli police. After an intense firefight that killed nine of the perpetrators, Prime Minister Ehud Barak announced the start of Operation Litani—an aggressive air-ground campaign to drive the PLO away from their sanctuaries along the Israel-Lebanon border. Thus began Israel's involvement in the Lebanese Civil War.

During this time of rising tension with Lebanon and the PLO, Israeli F-15s scored their first aerial victories on June 27, 1979. On that day, two Israeli flight groups—call-signed *Groom* and *Thames*—were covering an air strike against targets near Sidon and Tyre. *Groom* consisted of four Israeli F-15A fighters while *Thames* hosted two F-15A and two Israeli-built Kfir jets. As expected, the Syrian Air Force had dispatched their fighter squadrons to the region to intercept any lingering Israeli aircraft. Six MiG-21s took flight to intercept *Groom* and *Thames*, but when the Syrian MiGs identified the intruding aircraft as F-15s, they promptly disengaged. To lure the MiGs back to the battlefront, however, the attack formation initiated a fake bombing run while *Groom* and *Thames* flew southwest towards the Mediterranean coast. The tactical ploy worked and, when the MiG-21s reappeared, the Israeli F-15s vectored to intercept.

Locking on to the MiGs from a distance of ten miles, "Groom 2," "Groom 3," and "Groom 4" each fired an AIM-7 missile, all of which missed their targets. However, as the F-15s closed in, Groom 2 (piloted by Lieutenant Colonel Moshe Melnik) spotted a pair of MIG-21s crossing below his flight path at a distance of three miles. The MiGs began conducting evasive maneuvers just as Melnik launched his Python 3 missile, destroying the lead bandit and confirming the first aerial kill for an Israeli F-15.

Meanwhile, Groom 4 (piloted by Captain Joel Feldschuh) zeroed in on the surviving MiG, firing another AIM-7. Convinced that his AIM-7 would be a miss, Feldschuh prematurely fired his Sidewinder missile just as the AIM-7 began tracking the MiG, destroying the bandit and scoring the second Israeli kill for the afternoon.

After the two offending MiGs fell to Israeli fire, Thames 1 (piloted by Major Yoram Peled, whose father, Beni Peled, had test-flown the F-15 five years earlier) sighted two additional MiGs flying parallel to his left. With Thames 2 (flown by Major Guy Golan) covering his wing, Peled made a hard break towards the wayward MiGs.[1]

Groom 3 (piloted by Lieutenant Colonel Eitan Ben-Eliyahu), meanwhile, began chasing the same MiGs as they dove downward to avoid their F-15 pursuers. Ben-Eliyahu fired an AIM-7 at the leading MiG-21, but the missile stubbornly vectored off as the bandit rolled out from his dive. Yoram Peled, undeterred by his wingman's errant shot, fired his Sidewinder missile, scoring a direct hit on the leading MiG. As the lead bandit met his fiery fate, however, Ben-Eliyahu closed in on the trailing MiG.

Because the remaining bandit was too close for missiles, Ben-Eliyahu set his selector switch to "Guns." Picking up speed, the Israeli ace jettisoned his ventral tank and fired a 20mm cannon burst from a distance of 300 meters, sending the MiG's fiery carcass hurtling into the ground below. Towards the end of this melee, Thames 4 (Captain Shay Eshel) shot down a fifth MiG from aboard his domestically-built Kfir jet using a Python 3 missile, scoring the Kfir's first aerial kill.

Throughout Israel's involvement in the Lebanese Civil War, the Double Tail Squadron flew countless air patrols over the borderlands. It was during these regular flyovers in the summer of 1979 when Israeli F-15s once again met Syrian MiGs in the skies over Lebanon. After their initial skirmishes in June, the Syrian Air Force began flying closer to the Israeli border, hoping to bait the IDF into another air battle. As Syrian Defense Minister, Mustafa Tlas, justified it: "The decision to face the IDF is an important one for us to take. The enemy has repeatedly taken advantage of its air superiority in order to launch attacks that have killed many Arabs in Lebanon and forced many others to flee the country. Can we stand by and allow the enemy such freedom of action? Should we ground our fighters and restrain our heroic pilots, who are eager to engage the enemy

---

1. Three months after his successful encounter with the MiG-21s, Guy Golan was tragically killed on September 29, 1979 when his plane crashed en route from a mission over Lebanon.

An Israeli F–15 takes flight from Uvda Air Base during Operation Blue Flag, an annual, multi-national training exercise involving the air forces of the United States, Greece, Italy and Poland. (IDF)

despite the inevitable losses? Because these men are prepared to be victims for Syria in its ongoing struggle against Israel, the fighter pilots have continued to fly their missions." As these close encounters continued along the Lebanese border, Israeli F-15s scored more aerial victories against the antiquated MiG-21s—downing four in September 1979, and confirming an additional three kills in 1980. Indeed, by 1980, the F-15 Baz had achieved a kill-loss ratio of 9 to 0.

Israeli F-15s scored additional kills by the spring of 1981. For example, while flying wingman during one Combat Air Patrol, Captain Ilan Margalit discovered four Syrian MiG-21s attempting to intercept an Israeli F-4 Phantom performing reconnaissance. Margalit locked on one of the two leading MiG and launched his AIM-7F missile, scoring a direct hit.

After their latest defeats in the skies over Lebanon, the Syrian Air Force began the bitter task of rebuilding their battered air fleets. Sworn to vengeance, they acquired newer variants of the MiG-23 and MiG-25 for the next aerial showdown. The Israelis, meanwhile, were also rebuilding. By 1981, they had received more F-15s along with their first delivery of the new F-16 Fighting Falcon.

Although impressed by their string of victories, the IDF still had no indication of how the F-15 would fare in combat against the MiG-25 Foxbat. Although the Eagle had been built in response to the MiG-25 and its stable mates, NATO's intelligence community knew little about the Foxbat beyond its observable performance metrics. Even after Lieutenant Belenko's infamous defection aboard his MiG-25, Western analysts could not conclusively determine how their own fourth-generation fighters would fair in a dogfight against the Foxbat and its latter-day contemporaries. However, on February 13, 1981, any doubts about the Eagle's viability against the MiG-25 were quickly put to rest.

As it turned out, the Soviet Union had recently provided Syria with a small fleet of MiG-25s for reconnaissance and high-altitude interceptions. On that afternoon of February 13, an Israeli F-4 Phantom went aloft to conduct reconnaissance of the Lebanese borderlands when a Syrian MiG-25 vectored to intercept. To this point, Israeli

Displaying the roundel of the Israeli Air Force, two F-15s taxi down the runway at Uvda Air Base in southern Israel. (IDF)

F-4s had been running regular reconnaissance missions over the borderland, where they were frequently targeted by marauding MiG-21s and MiG-23s. Although these recon variants of the F-4 were regarded as "easy prey," they never went aloft without a fully-armed, multi-layered Combat Air Patrol (CAP) nearby. But even without a fighter escort, the typical Israeli F-4 could climb faster than the MiG-21 and easily outmaneuver a MiG-23.

Today, however, this F-4 would be targeted by a Syrian MiG-25.

Leading the CAP in support of this F-4's recon mission was Lieutenant Colonel Benny Zinker—commander of the Double Tail Squadron. Because weather conditions were poor that day, neither Zinker nor his wingmen expected the Syrians to intercept the reconnaissance flight. Nevertheless, the Israelis' radar soon populated with the signature of an enemy plane.

General David Ivry, the Israeli Air Force Commander, recalled that "the Syrian fighter was flying an interception course, accelerating very fast." From the relative speed of the radar blip, he could tell that the incoming fighter was either a MiG-23 or a MiG-25. Zinker and his wingmen were flying over the Sea of Galilee when they were alerted that the Syrian fighter had been scrambled to intercept. Simultaneously, Israeli ground control ordered the F-4 to abort its mission while Zinker vectored his F-15 to meet the lingering bogey.

Acquiring the bandit on his radar, Zinker fired an AIM-7 Sparrow missile from a distance of 25 miles, and launched a second Sparrow only moments later. After a few more moments, Zinker launched a third AIM-7 missile and watched in delight as the amorphous bandit exploded in a flash of light. Zinker saw debris from the enemy fuselage falling to the Earth, but he couldn't determine if the bandit had been a MiG-23 or MiG-25.

By now, however, Zinker had wandered into Syrian airspace—and beat a hasty retreat before any other MiGs could arrive on the scene. Two weeks later, the Syrian government confirmed that the lost aircraft had indeed been a MiG-25. It was the first time in history that a Foxbat had been bested by enemy fire.

Five months later, on July 29, 1981, Israeli F-15s once again proved their mettle against the MiG-25. After a fragile cease-fire had been declared between Syria and Israel, the latter stated they would still be flying reconnaissance missions over Lebanon's border. Israeli Prime Minister, Menachem Begin, defended the recon flights, stating: "We have to carry out the overflights to know what is going on and to find out where there are

After achieving air superiority over the Mediterranean with the F-15 "Baz," the Israeli Air Force solicited the US for a ground-attack variant of the F-15. Consequently, the Israelis received the F-15E Strike Eagle, re-christening it the "Ra'am"—Hebrew for "thunder." (IDF)

the PLO's bases…"

Israel claimed it was a matter of preventive defense—lest the PLO use the cease-fire as a pretext to re-arm their border camps. On July 29, another Israeli F-4 took flight on a reconnaissance mission when two Syrian MiG-21s and two MiG-25s scrambled to intercept. Almost on cue, a flight of F-15s from the Double Tail Squadron vectored to fight off the incoming Syrian bandits. Within moments of arriving on the scene, the F-15 piloted by Major Shaul Simon acquired radar lock on the leading MiG-25, and fired off an AIM-7 missile. The Arab Foxbat exploded into a giant fireball—a sight that sent his now-rattled wingmen into retreat. Indeed, the remaining MiGs had no desire to tussle with the F-15. When Syria threatened to shoot down any further reconnaissance flights, Prime Minister Begin replied:

"It is easier said than done, because today we have shot down a MiG-25."

Following another cease-fire in July 1981, the Israeli Air Force and its F-15s saw little action until May 1982. In their latest round of hostility, PLO forces initiated a 12-day artillery attack on Galilee in northern Israel. By the end of the bombardment, sixty Israeli civilians had been killed. But as the Israeli government contemplated its response, their ambassador to the United Kingdom, Shlomo Argov, was brutally shot in the head during an assassination attempt on June 3, 1982. Argov survived the attack, but the gunshot left him paralyzed for the remainder of his life. Israel concluded that the assassination attempt had been part of a PLO conspiracy in combination with the attack on Galilee. The following day, Israel declared the start of "Operation Peace for Galilee"—a full-scale invasion of Lebanon.

On June 6, 1982, seven Israeli divisions—including 60,000 troops and 500 tanks—crossed into southern Lebanon. The IDF had planned the invasion as a three-pronged attack—with air and ground forces deploying along the coastline, the central mountains, and an area known as the Bekaa Valley near the Syrian border.

Occupying the Bekaa Valley was pivotal for success—and the IDF was hoping that Syria wouldn't get involved. These hopes were quickly dashed, however, when Syrian MiGs appeared along the Lebanese border, trying to engage Israeli aircraft. But as before, the Syrian MiGs proved no match for the Israeli F-15s. For on June 7, 1982, Israeli pilot Aharon Lapidot scored the first aerial kill of the Lebanon War.

Flying an F-15 call-signed "Baz 658," Lapidot reflected on the engagement as such:

"We were on a CAP south of Beirut. The Syrian IADS [air defense network] was still intact, and it covered all the area from the Lebanese-Syrian border in the east up to the ridge of the Lebanon Mountains in the west. This meant that in order to stay outside of the IADS' engagement envelope, yet still provide cover for the strike aircraft, we had to patrol over the coast. We received plenty of warning about SyAAF [Syrian Air Force] aircraft both from our fighter controllers and the radar screens in our jets. A threat got too close to our attack aircraft and we were vectored in to protect them. The weather was cloudy below us, and we stayed above the undercast throughout the mission.

For some reason that I cannot now recall, my four-ship formation—in which I

Under a moonlit night, three Israeli F-15s stand on the tarmac in Decimommanu, Sardinia. As a part of the IDF's delegation to the island of Sardinia, these F-15s were participating in aerial drills over the Mediterranean Sea. (IDF)

was No. 4—lost the target aircraft that had initially been vectored onto. When we reached the boundary of the IADS engagement envelope we turned back. Just as I completed my turn to the west and the Syrian pilot turned from west to north. I locked my radar onto the MiG-23 and stated over the radio that I had positive identification, and that I was about to launch an AAM. I duly fired an AIM-7F seconds later.

The greatest problem facing my squadron during the war was the correct identification of aircraft that we encountered north of the border. The informal order that we obeyed within the unit was that no one was to open fire without first achieving a positive identification of the target. This was just as well, for later in the war I intercepted a jet and the GCU cleared me to fire an AAM, but I chose not to launch the missile. This was a wise move, as it turned out that my 'target' was an IDF/AF aircraft!

The Sparrow failed to hit the MiG-23, despite it meeting all the required acquisition parameters that included the target being well within its engagement envelope. By the time I realized that I had missed, I was within Python 3 range of the jet. I therefore fired a single WVR AAM [air-to-air missile] at a distance of 1.5 miles whilst flying at an altitude of 1,000–2,000 ft in a look-down position on the MiG, which made it more difficult for the missile to track its target. Soon after firing the weapon I turned sharply to the east in order to avoid any SAMs, or engagement with the MiG-23's wingman. This in turn meant that I did not see the AAM hit the target. Other pilots in formation saw the kill, however."

The battle raged hard and fast—becoming somewhat of a legend in the history of the IDF. But Prime Minister Begin, determined to prove that this was a conflict *exclusively* between Israel and Lebanon, appealed to Syrian President Hafez al-Assad, urging Syria not to intervene. On June 8, in an address to the Israeli Parliament, Begin said:

> "I once again state that we do not want a war with Syria. From this platform, I call on President Assad to instruct the Syrian army not to harm Israeli soldiers and then nothing bad will happen to them [Syrian soldiers]. We desire no clashes with the Syrian army. If we reach the line 40 kilometers from our northern border the work will have been done, all fighting will end. I am directing my words to the ears of the President of Syria. He knows how to keep an agreement. He signed a cease-fire with us and kept it. He did not allow the terrorists to act. If he behaves in this manner now in Lebanon, no Syrian soldier will be harmed by our soldiers."

Syria, however, didn't heed the Prime Minister's warning.

The following day—June 9, 1982—Operation "Mole Cricket 19" commenced. Leading the operation was Israeli Air Force Commander, General David Ivry. He later confirmed that although Israel did not want war with Syria, their anti-aircraft sites in Lebanon still had to be destroyed. The biggest challenge, however, was the constrictive airspace of the Bekaa Valley and the surrounding area. In fact, the usable airspace was barely 1,500 square miles—an area that was sure to be crowded. Ivry noted that "sometimes we had more than 100 planes flying in this kind of environment."

With the goal of destroying twenty surface-to-air missile (SAM) locations, Ivry ordered the strike missions to begin at 2:00 PM local time. In a manner similar to the ground assault, the Israeli Air Force developed a three-pronged attack. First, the Israelis' Remotely-Piloted Vehicles (RPVs) flew in to divert the attention of the Syrians' air defense radars. Simultaneously, the RPVs sent video footage back to Israeli ground control. Next, Israeli F-4 Phantoms took on the primary role of attacking the SAMs, firing off high-speed, anti-radiation missiles. Finally, covering the entire area for interception and air-to-air combat were the Israeli F-15s and F-16s. Twenty minutes into the assault, however, Syrian jets took flight to intercept the Israelis.

But just as before, the Syrian MiGs stood no chance.

Veteran pilot Moshe Melnik, who had scored the inaugural kill for the F-15 three years earlier, flew the opening sortie for Operation "Peace for Galilee." He recalled the opening volleys as such: "We kept the Syrians from flying in Lebanon, and did it in the best possible fashion. Every flight of Syrian planes that tried to cross the lines and attack our forces in Lebanon was shot down. Sometimes a single plane out of the flight escaped and told the others the story of what had happened. We had a field day, basically, shooting down practically everything that flew. The MiG-21 and MiG-23, which formed the backbone of the Syrian air force, were crushed. As far as our squadron was concerned, the war was more like a shooting range." Indeed, it later became known as the "Bekaa Valley Turkey Shoot."

Two hours later, all SAM locations had been destroyed without the loss of a single Israeli jet. General Ivry reflected that the mission had been a success due to the extensive planning, superior tactics, and superior equipment. As Ivry recalled, the MiG pilots were

Three F-15s in fly-by formation during Israel's Independence Day celebration, 2017. (Minusig)

"not very efficient" in intercepting the F-15s. In fact, by Ivry's estimate, the Israelis shot down nearly seventy-five percent of the Syrian aircraft involved in the operation. "And the more they came," he said, "the lack of confidence on their side was increased. Once you start to lose, you think, 'Well, I'm going to be a target, and I'm going to go over there because I've been summoned.' I can only tell you that, within half an hour, we shot down about 26 MiGs."

Although the SAM sites had been neutralized, the operation was far from over. During the next forty-eight hours, the Syrian Air Force dispatched nearly 100 aircraft—mostly MiG-23s, MiG-25s, and Su-20s—to intercept the Israeli F-15s.

Aside from the F-15's superior capabilities, the Israelis' comparative radar techniques gave them a significant advantage. Indeed, the Israeli pilots were being guided by E-2C Airborne Warning and Control System (AWACS) planes flying from beyond the range of Syria's missile sites. The Syrian MiG-21s and MiG-23s, on the other hand, were using Ground Controlled Interception (GCI) to find the Israeli F-15 and F-16s. GCI consisted of ground-based radar stations which guided the intercepting aircraft to its target in the sky. The problem with GCI, however, was that the radar stations could easily be jammed—thereby cutting off communication with the planes, and rendering their pilots blind.

The mobile E-2C AWACS, however, were far less susceptible to the same jamming techniques. To boot, the F-15 Eagle and F-16 Fighting Falcon both had powerful, long-range onboard radars that, likewise, were not as susceptible to jamming. Try as they may, the Syrians simply couldn't match the multi-layered situational awareness of the Israeli Air Force. As one Syrian pilot stated: "When we closed to 10-15km (6-9 miles) to the enemy, our radars would go black and we would lose all means of detecting them. Heavy jamming wasn't concentrated on our radars alone, but also on our communications with ground control."

Meanwhile, during the opening volleys of the air campaign, the Israeli F-15s in CAP

An F-15I Ra'am from the 69 Squadron prepares to take off from Hatzerim Air Base. Although not as celebrated as its air superiority "Baz" cousin, the "Ra'am" is nevertheless projected to have a long service life in the Israeli Air Force. (IDF)

formation positively identified a MIG-23 closing in from a distance of five to seven miles. Acquiring missile lock, one Baz pilot fired his AIM-7F. Seconds after firing, he watched helplessly as the missile careened away from its target. The angry MiG-23 locked on him instead. But rather than retreat, the F-15 pilot fired his Python 3 missile from a distance of one-and-a-half miles. As the missile glided away from its rail, the Baz pilot noticed the incoming missile that the MiG pilot had simultaneously fired at him.

The Israeli pilot successfully evaded the Syrian missile but the MiG-23 wasn't so lucky. Indeed, the Python missile made its impact squarely into the fuselage of the wayward MiG, confirming Israel's first air-to-air victory of the Lebanon War.

Moments later, Captain Yoram Hoffman and Major Ronen Shapira went into action against incoming MiG-21s. Hoffman was flying wingman to the flight leader when he spotted the MiG coming in from a low altitude. Positively identifying the bogey as a MiG-21, Hoffman acquired radar lock and hastily defeated the MiG with a missile shot. Shapira, meanwhile, noticed another MiG-21 closing in from the rear. Performing a "high-G" turn, Shapira maneuvered his plane into the six o'clock position. Firing off an AIM-7, Shapira winced in frustration as the missile failed to hit its target. Undeterred, Shapira quickly hit the selector switch for his Python 3 missile, servicing the target and destroying the MiG with a direct hit.

June 10, 1982 was the busiest day for Israel's F-15 squadrons. By now, the Double Tail Squadron was providing fighter escort for aerial missions all over Lebanon. On this day alone, Israeli fighters shot down *thirteen* Syrian MiGs. Astonishingly, three of these air-to-air victories were accomplished by just *one* pilot—Avner Naveh, piloting Baz 957 over the Lebanon Valley, just south of the Beirut-Damascus highway. Naveh single-handedly shot down two MiG-23s and a MiG-21. This accomplishment made him the first F-15 "ace"—a term bestowed upon any pilot with five or more kills. Naveh was also the first F-15 pilot to score three kills during a single sortie. Later that day, Captain Ziv Nadivi, flying Baz 848, shot down a Gazelle helicopter with a Python 3 missile—one of only two confirmed helicopter kills during the Lebanon War.

The Syrians, meanwhile, tried to stem the tide of Israeli air power. Sending their MiGs and Sukhois over Beirut, the Syrian Air Force continued to fly what remained of their fledgling fleet. All told, however, they were simply no match for the Israeli Air Force, due in no small part to their superior air capabilities and radar technology.

On the last day of the war—June 11, 1982—there was limited action, but the F-15 squadrons nevertheless confirmed five additional kills. Two of them were recorded by Major Yoram Peled, giving him five confirmed kills as well, and making him the second ace alongside Avner Naveh. Yoram Peled's first kill of the day occurred when flying alongside Moshe Melnik as part of a 4-plane sortie taking off from Tel Nof Air Base. As Melnik and Peled flew across the mountain tops of the Lebanon Valley, they noted four MiGs approaching. Performing a defensive split, Peled killed two bandits—one with a Sparrow missile; the other with his Python 3.

On the way back to Tel Nof, however, Peled and Melnik were caught by two marauding MiG-21s. The lead MiG fired a volley of missiles at the Israeli patrol, none of which met their mark. Melnik, however, returned the favor with a Python 3 missile—skillfully downing the lead bandit with a direct hit. Meanwhile, Captain Avi Maor went after the second MiG, destroying it with a quick burst from his 20mm autocannon.

By the end of its 8-day war, the Israel Air Force claimed 88 kills, with 13 losses—none of which were F-15s. Of the 88 confirmed kills, 33 were credited to the F-15 squadrons. Israeli losses included one F-16, one F-4 Phantom, one Kfir jet, and ten helicopters.

In the summer of 1982, Israel received another delivery of F-15s. The new arrivals were upgraded models—F-15C and D variants. In total, the Israeli Air Force received 18 C-variants and 8 D-variants during this time. With a larger fleet, the Israeli Air Force began evaluating the F-15 for roles beyond air-to-air combat. Responding to the air power that Israel had demonstrated during the Lebanon War, the surrounding countries began investing heavily in surface-to-surface missile (SSM) technology. Ballistic missiles, they reasoned, could possibly mitigate the need to fight Israel in the sky. With new SSM capabilities, the Arab states could attack Israel from within the sanctuary of their own borders. As the Arabs aggressively built their arsenal of Soviet-built SSMs, the Israelis pondered whether the F-15 could be adapted into a "strike aircraft," capable of ground attack missions.

The Israeli Air Force began training their fighter cadres in the tactics of air-to-ground warfare, but the F-15 was, by design, never intended to be an attack aircraft. "Not one pound for air-to-ground" had been the popular mantra within McDonnell Douglas. Despite its conception as a pure air superiority fighter, the Israelis found that the F-15 Baz could be easily adapted for ground attack missions.

Although these air-to-ground capabilities had heretofore been based on theory and

An Israeli F-15D crew stops for refueling in the Azores Islands, en route to Mountain Home Air Force Base, Idaho. Upon arriving in the US, the crew will be participating in their annual joint-exercises with the US Air Force. (IDF)

training experiments, the Israeli F-15s decisively proved their ground-attack prowess in the fall of 1985. On September 25 of that year, during Yom Kippur, three Palestinian gunmen hijacked an Israeli yacht off the coast of Cyprus, killing three Israeli tourists on board. Not surprisingly, evidence pointed to the PLO, seemingly in retaliation for the imprisonment of a local commander. Shocked by the nature of these dastardly murders, the Israeli government decided to target the PLO headquarters, located in Tunis, Tunisia—a port city on the coast of the Mediterranean.

The attack was to be prompt and secretive. On October 1, 1985, six Israeli F-15Ds and two F-15Cs took flight from Tel Nof Airbase, en route to Tunis. The mission had been dubbed Operation "Wooden Leg"—the longest-range airstrike in Israeli history. Accompanying the F-15s into battle were two KC-707s for aerial refueling. The distance of the strike was made longer by the fact that it had to be completed without being detected by the Syrian, Tunisian, or Egyptian radar networks.

The mission objective was simple: destroy the PLO headquarters. This ground-attack mission, however, was something that the F-15 had never done. Some within the IDF wondered if the F-15 Baz could fly such a great distance and remain undetected. There was also the question of armament accuracy. By 1985, precision-guided munitions were still in their infancy, and the Israelis were unsure of how the 2,000-pound GBU-15 glide bombs would perform at lower altitudes.

As the first three F-15Ds descended onto the coastal city, the pilots deployed their GBU-15 bombs, all of which scored direct hits on the PLO compound. Following suit, the three remaining F-15Ds dropped their own GBU-15s—again scoring direct hits on the PLO headquarters. Finally, the two F-15Cs scored hits with their own precision-guided bombs. The PLO headquarters complex was completely destroyed, although the PLO leader, Yasser Arafat, had not been present during the attack. Approximately sixty PLO personnel died in the attack—including several of Arafat's bodyguards. Additionally, dozens of civilian bystanders perished during the attack. According to other sources, fifty-six Palestinians and sixteen Tunisians were killed, with more than 100 wounded.

Operation Wooden Leg lasted a mere six minutes, after which the F-15s returned to Tel Nof Airbase unscathed.

Although the Israeli government stood by its actions, claiming that the attack had been in retaliation for the PLO's aggression in Cyprus, the United Nations condemned the operation. Although the international community debated Israel's justification for the attack, there could be little debate that the F-15 was now a viable ground-attack aircraft.

Beyond Operation Wooden Leg, the F-15 Baz would see little action. In fact, the Baz scored its final kill to date on November 19, 1985. During a routine reconnaissance mission over Lebanon, a flight of Israeli F-15s were engaged by a pair of MiG-23s. The F-15s gave chase, downing both bandits with their Python 3 missiles.

Despite the lack of further combat, the Israeli Air Force continued to purchase additional F-15s throughout the 1990s. Then, in 1997, Israel announced the arrival of its newest variant - the F-15I, nicknamed "Ra'am" (Hebrew for *thunder*). The Ra'am was based on the F-15E Strike Eagle—the two-seated, ground-attack variant of the air superiority F-15. Having seen the Strike Eagle's performance during the 1991 Gulf War, the Israeli Air Force purchased several variants to supplement their ground attack squadrons. To this point, the Israelis had been using the F-15C and D-variants for air-to-ground missions, but the IDF was excited to have a specially-modified F-15 that was built to accommodate that role.

After approaching McDonnell Douglas and the Department of Defense, Israel ordered twenty-five F-15Es and made further arrangements for Israeli Aerospace Industries (IAI) to assist in modifying and updating the onboard avionics. Israel wanted to be more involved in updating the Strike Eagle. Having worked with the F-15 so long, they knew what modifications would best suit the Israeli Air Force. Major upgrades included a new central computer, GPS navigational systems, and an Elbit display and sight helmet (DASH). For its armament, the F-15I could still accommodate the existing inventory of Sparrow and Sidewinder missiles. But now, the Ra'am could carry the AIM-120—an American missile that could be fired from well beyond visual sight range. And because the F-15I had been fitted for ground attack missions, the Ra'am would also house 36 Rockeye cluster bombs and six Maverick air-to-ground missiles. Later still, the F-15I would add the Paveway laser-guided bombs, Joint Direct Attack Munition (JDAM) satellite-guided bombs, BLUE-109 "bunker-buster" bombs, and the AGM-88 HARM anti-radar missile to its onboard arsenal.

Today, the F-15 remains in service with the Israeli Air Force. Throughout its history in the service of Judea, the F-15 has proven itself a reliable and resilient weapon in the face of Arab aggression. In aerial skirmishes across the Mediterranean, Israeli pilots reinforced the legend and mystique of the F-15 around the world. That the F-15 Baz and F-15I Ra'am remain in active service is a testament to the quality of their design.

Thunder in the Gulf

In the summer of 1990, mankind stood on the brink of a new era. Gone were the days of the Cold War—the Iron Curtain had fallen and the once-mighty Soviet Union lay on its deathbed. After nearly fifty years of ideological struggle, the United States stood as the world's lone superpower. But as Communism disappeared from Eastern Europe, and America reaped the benefits of her "peace dividend," a new conflict loomed on the horizon.

On the morning of August 2, 1990, Iraqi forces under the command of Saddam Hussein invaded the tiny emirate of Kuwait. Within hours, the Kuwaiti defenses collapsed under the onslaught of the Iraqi Army. The invasion drew fierce condemnation from

American F-15 pilots from the 58th Fighter Squadron prepare to deploy to Operation Desert Shield, 1990. In response to the Kuwaiti invasion, the US military deployed forces to Saudi Arabia, lest Saddam Hussein invade the Kingdom of Saud. (US Air Force)

the international community and prompted the United Nations to demand Saddam's withdrawal. Undeterred by the rhetoric, the Iraqi dictator massed his forces along the Saudi Arabian border and dared the world to stop him.

Saddam was certain that his army—the fourth-largest in the world and equipped with the latest in Soviet armor—would make short order of any rescue force that came to liberate Kuwait. He wagered that the Americans would lead a military response against Iraq but, as he famously quipped, America was "a society that cannot accept 10,000 dead in one battle." Indeed, the memories of Vietnam were as galvanizing to Saddam Hussein as they were disheartening to the American public. He was confident that after the Americans had suffered a few thousand casualties, they would sue for peace on Iraq's terms. But for as fearsome as Saddam's army sounded, his air force was primitive by NATO standards. Although the Iraqi Air Force possessed the MiG-25 and MiG-29, the Iraqis had no viable air defense grid—a mistake that would cost them dearly in the opening days of the air campaign.

Saddam Hussein rose to power in 1968 following the Ba'ath Party revolution. However, as he ascended to the presidency, Saddam ruled Iraq with a brand of brutality reminiscent of Hitler and Stalin. Consolidating his power into a dictatorship, he seemed poised for a long, prosperous rule of Iraq…until his fortunes changed in the wake of the Iranian Revolution.

Fearful that the Ayatollah's rhetoric would galvanize Iraq's Shiite majority, Saddam preemptively invaded Iran on October 22, 1980. The ensuing Iran-Iraq War lasted eight years and ended in a bloody stalemate that claimed more than 300,000 Iraqi dead. Aside from the untold cost in human suffering, the conflict left Saddam straddled with a multi-billion-dollar war debt, most of which had been financed by Kuwait. But rather than pay his debt to the Kuwaiti government, the "Butcher of Baghdad" simply invaded his neighbor to the south. To justify the invasion, Saddam reignited the long-standing border dispute between the two countries. He also made false allegations that the Kuwaitis had been slant-drilling Iraqi oil and that they were deliberately trying to keep the price of oil low by producing beyond OPEC's set quotas. Kuwait held ten percent of the world's oil reserves and generated 97 billion barrels of crude each year. Thus, Saddam reasoned that if he could not pay repay his debt, he would simply annex the tiny emirate and take over its petroleum industry.

Thus, on the morning of August 2, more than 100,000 Iraqi troops and several hundred Iraqi tanks stormed across the border, the spearhead of an eighty-mile blitzkrieg into Kuwait City. Encountering only piecemeal resistance, Iraqi tanks thundered into the heart of the Kuwaiti capital, assaulting the city's central bank and carrying off with its wealth. A coordinated air-ground attack decimated the Dasman Palace, home to Kuwait's ruler Emir Jabel al-Amhad al-Sabar. The emir and a few members of his staff barely escaped with their lives as they fled Kuwait by helicopter. The last transmission made over the state-run radio network was an appeal for help.

The United Nations responded with their normal variety of condemnations. Economic and military sanctions soon followed while President George Bush authorized the first US deployments to the region. Within days, the aircraft carriers *Saratoga* and *Eisenhower* were steaming towards the Persian Gulf while coalition air squadrons began pouring

F–15Cs from the 58th Fighter Squadron prepare to take flight from Eglin Air Force Base, Florida, en route to Saudi Arabia, 1990. (US Air Force)

into Saudi Arabia by the hundreds. The first wave of deployments became known as "Operation Desert Shield"—a deterrent against Saddam Hussein lest he try to invade the Kingdom of Saud.

Among the first air squadrons to arrive in the Persian Gulf were the 336 Tactical Fighter Squadron and the 58th Tactical Fighter Squadron. Following suit were the 60th Tactical Fighter Squadron (the vaunted "Fighting Crows"), the 53rd Tactical Fighter Squadron; and the 525th Tactical Fighter Squadron. Collectively, these fighter squadrons arrived with contingents of F-15C, F-15D, and F-15E Strike Eagles.

As the military coalition grew, Lieutenant General Chuck Horner (USAF) became the commander of Allied air forces. At his command were more than 2,500 tactical aircraft—1,800 of which were American. The remainder came from a smattering of allies including France, Canada, and the United Kingdom. It was, by all measures, the largest aggregate air force since World War II.

Although Saddam's air squadrons were numerically inferior to the UN coalition, the Iraqis still possessed more than 500 Soviet-built aircraft. Coalition air forces may have had Saddam outnumbered, but his pilots (many of whom were veterans of the Iran-Iraq War), would undoubtedly defend the skies of Iraq unto to their deaths.

In the opening months of Operation Desert Shield, American F-15 pilots flew aerial maneuvers similar to what they would experience in combat. However, US Central Command Air Forces (CENTAF) initially kept their F-15s on a tight leash. Indeed, after grounding all pilots during the first few weeks of Desert Shield, CENTAF subsequently limited their training sorties to a minimum altitude of 300 feet.

Meanwhile, CENTAF and coalition leaders created the Tactical Air Command Centre (TACC) to plan and organize the air campaign against Iraq. The forthcoming tactics, techniques, and procedures were eventually outlined in a 600-page document known as the "Air Tasking Order" (ATO). Among its many pages and annexes, the ATO included maps of aerial routes, lists of anticipated targets, and target arrival times. According to TACC, the F-15E would work in concert with the F-4G Wild Weasel and the EF-111 to destroy Iraqi missile sites and key airfields. Likewise, the F-15C and D-variant would fly alongside their stablemates—the F-14 Tomcat and F/A-18 Hornet—to clear the sky of any Iraqi MiGs.

In November 1990, as coalition air forces continued pouring into Saudi Arabia, the UN Security Council passed Resolution 678. The resolution, for what it was worth, gave Saddam Hussein a deadline of January 15 to withdraw his forces, or face military action. Still, the Iraqi dictator showed no signs of backing down. Thus, it came as no surprise when, on January 15, 1991, Saddam reached his deadline and made no effort to withdraw from Kuwait. Instead, the Butcher of Baghdad flexed his muscles and dared the world to stop him. The next day, President George Bush announced the start of the military campaign to eject the Iraqis from the war-torn emirate.

Operation Desert Shield had just become Operation Desert Storm.

On January 17, at 2:38 AM, Baghdad time, the first wave of the coalition's air campaign destroyed Iraqi radar sites near the Saudi border.

In the early morning hours of January 17, Captain Jon Kelk (callsign: "JB") achieved the first air-to-air victory of Desert Storm, as well as the first kill for an American F-15. By the dawn of Desert Shield, Jon Kelk was already an accomplished aviator—he had logged more than 2,000 flight hours aboard the Eagle and was a graduate of the prestigious Fighter Weapons School (F-15 Division). He arrived in Saudi Arabia with the 58th Fighter Squadron as part of the initial deployment of American forces to Desert Shield. Flying alongside Kelk during this first day of the air campaign was Captain Rob Graeter (callsign: "Cheese"). Like Kelk, Graeter was also an accomplished aviator—honing his skills as a member of the 65th Aggressor Squadron at Nellis Air Force Base, Nevada. Arriving at the 58th Fighter Squadron in 1989, Graeter was one of the designated mission commanders for the initial foray into Iraqi airspace.

Kelk and Greater found themselves assigned, respectively, to two different flight groups—codenamed *Pennzoil* and *Citgo*. The *Pennzoil* flight was an 8-plane formation led by Captain Rick "Kluso" Tollini. As Kelk recalled, during the lead-up to Desert Storm, it was decided that "Rick and I would alternate between leading the flight and flying the number three position." Essentially, Kelk and Tollini would take turns commanding the various sorties assigned to the 58th. Meanwhile, Rob Graeter would command the *Citgo* flight—a 4-plane formation. Both *Pennzoil* and *Citgo* would fly together into the opening melee against the Iraqi Air Force.

As Kelk recalled, "the big unknown was the capability and response of the Iraqi Air Force. If you just look at it on paper, it was a formidable force in terms of total numbers of fighter aircraft. We knew a lot about their air defense capabilities, and we had no intention or desire of flying through known SAM sites. As pure air-to-air guys, our goal was to engage anyone that got airborne and attempted to challenge the 'surprise attack'

F-15E Strike Eagles from the 4th Tactical Fighter Wing, shortly after arriving in Saudi Arabia, 1990. The F-15E Strike Eagle was distinguishable from the F-15A and F-15C by its darker body paint and two-seat configuration. (US Department of Defense)

of F-117s [Stealth Fighter] and F-15Es. The game plan was for the stealth guys to go in high and the F-15Es to go in low first, accomplish the surprise attack, and be out of Iraqi airspace before we pushed in to take out any enemy fighters."

All told, Kelk and Graeter expected to encounter a few MiG-25s and MiG-29s. By 1991, most of the Western world knew that the MiG-25 was fast, but substandard as a dogfighter. The MiG-29, however, was a different story. The last of the latter-day Soviet fighters, the MiG-29 was purportedly capable of fighting toe-to-toe against any fighter in NATO's inventory. Come what may, Kelk, Graeter, and their comrades of *Pennzoil* and

Citgo were prepared to take on the Iraqi airmen.

As the two flight groups ventured into Iraqi airspace, Kelk reviewed the mission plan in his head. The F-117 Nighthawks were to destroy the Iraqi Command and Control nodes in and around Baghdad, the F-15Es were to bomb the Scud missile sites and other air defense targets throughout Western Iraq. "The theory," Kelk said, "was that the F-117s would be invisible, and the F-15Es would be below Iraqi radar coverage." It was hoped that these initial bombing runs would trigger a response from Iraqi fighter-interceptors, at which time the regular F-15 Eagles like Kelk's would vector to destroy the enemy bandits.

At 3:00 AM local time, Kelk and his wingmen in the *Pennzoil* flight were waiting to rendezvous with *Citgo* when an urgent radio call arrived from a nearby AWACS. As it turned out, the AWACS's radar had detected enemy MiGs within striking distance of the F-117s and F-15Es—and subsequently ordered *Pennzoil* to intercept.

This early call was problematic for two reasons.

First, intercepting the Iraqi aircraft this early—while the F-117s and F-15Es were still in the area—would make for some *very* crowded airspace, thereby increasing the probability of fratricide. Second, Kelk and his comrades had expected to cover a 100-mile front alongside Graeter's *Citgo* formation. But as of now, the *Citgo* flight was still more than 100 miles south of *Pennzoil*. Realizing that they couldn't wait for *Citgo's* arrival, the *Pennzoil* F-15s vectored to intercept the incoming bandits.

Pushing forward into a linear "wall formation," Kelk and his *Pennzoil* wingmen flew northward, scanning their radars and listening intently to the radio traffic. "The radios got very busy on the strike frequency," he recalled, "and it was hard to get a word in edgewise."

Suddenly, Kelk's radar showed the blip of an incoming aircraft.

A bandit?—he wondered.

At a distance of 40 miles north, and an altitude of 7,000 feet, its relative position indicated that it was likely an enemy bandit. "I tried to get the AWACS to confirm… but had no luck. I was still very concerned about frat [fratricide], but even without the AWAC's help, I was confident that this was a bad guy. He was heading south towards me and climbing." Indeed, by the time Kelk readied his first missile, the bandit was at 17,000 feet. "Once I was in parameters," he said, "I fired a single AIM-7." As soon as Kelk depressed the trigger, he closed his eyes, not wanting the white flash the missile to rob him of his night vision. "We had flown a lot of nights during the pre-war time in Saudi and were very good at flying nights in the pre-NVG [night vision goggles] era, and I didn't want to risk it."

After deploying his missile, however, Kelk was unsure of whether the AIM-7 had met its target. "I look out the front and I see a purple-blueish light on the horizon"—not the telltale orange fireball he had been expecting. "After about three to five seconds, it fades." Kelk was bewildered.

Did he kill the bandit?

Was this purple-blue ember the skewed sight of an explosion?

Had the enemy bandit been dropping flares?

"At night, you can't judge the distance, he said, "so I just wasn't certain." He did a radar search of the immediate area and found nothing.

Whoever this bandit may have been, he had now disappeared from radar view.

To make matters worse, the instrumentation aboard Kelk's F-15 was malfunctioning. As was customary, Kelk was expected to jettison his external fuel tanks upon end-of-mission. The tanks, however, refused to come off. The additional weight would undoubtedly slow him down when the rest of the *Pennzoil* formation sallied back into Saudi airspace. Adding to the confusion was the onboard weapons panel. Despite having fired an AIM-7 missile, the panel showed that all missiles were still attached to Kelk's wings.

"I guess were about 75 miles south of Baghdad at this time," said Kelk. Although he had indeed fired a missile, he was unsure whether he had truly killed the faceless bandit. "I didn't call the splash for several reasons," he said. "The radios were still real busy, and I was more concerned with the next merge [rendezvous] than making a radio call. Also, with the conflicting cockpit indications I had been getting, I didn't feel that I was in a place to make that call." However, after Pennzoil had re-grouped and was back over Saudi airspace, Kelk called out to his wingman, Captain Mark Williams, to visually inspect his missile rack. Flying alongside Kelk's wing, Williams confirmed that the AIM-7 was missing—the weapons panel was wrong; Kelk had indeed fired the AIM-7.

Back at the Tabuk airbase, and still unsure of his aerial victory, Kelk reported it as a "probable" kill. A few hours later, however, the AWACS that had been aloft with *Pennzoil* sent its report to Kelk's squadron commander. Not only had Kelk destroyed the bandit, the kill had been confirmed as a MiG-29.

While Jon Kelk had been tussling with the MiG-29 (and his own malfunctioning instruments), Rob Graeter and his comrades in the *Citgo* flight had been exceptionally busy. Flying lead for the formation, "my flight was the first off the runaway," said Graeter. After an in-flight refueling from a nearby aerotanker, *Citgo* deployed into a Combat Air Patrol formation between 60-80 nautical miles south of the Iraqi border. Because their mission's designated start time was still 45 minutes away, this gave the *Citgo* airmen "plenty of time to relax and get set up," recalled Graeter.

Listening on the radio, Graeter heard the same call from the nearby AWACS, ordering *Pennzoil* to intercept the incoming flight of MiGs. In the same transmission, the AWACS commander ordered *Citgo* to likewise push northward. Like Kelk, Graeter realized that the early call would disrupt their erstwhile plans to engage enemy aircraft as a 100-mile front. In Graeter's words, the early push rendered Pennzoil and Citgo into a "60-mile echelon southwest formation." Graeter later recalled that the premature deployment had "really screwed us up." For according to Graeter: "We would have had a much better picture if we had waited, since the idea was to get the MiGs airborne off their alert pads, chasing the strikers."

Still, Graeter and the rest of the *Citgo* flight group made the best of the situation and acknowledged the AWACS's call. According to the AWACS, the incoming bandits were MiG-29s, far north of Iraq's Mudaysis Airbase. Graeter "rogered" the call, but because the MiGs were more than 100 miles north, he could not yet see them on his own radar. As *Citgo* pressed north towards the border, however, Graeter detected the egressing F-15E Strike Eagles. In fact, the Strike Eagles had just cleared their target areas.

Therein, however, lay the problem with *Pennzoil's* and *Citgo's* early push.

Indeed, the airspace would be considerably crowded—having "good guys mixed in

Airmen assigned to the 1st Tactical Fighter Wing fill sandbags to create a protective barrier around the unit's F-15Cs. (US Air Force)

with bad guys." According to Graeter, the original mission plan was to be able to shoot from beyond visual range within a relatively clear airspace.

As Graeter drove towards the Strike Eagles' egress corridor, the AWACS alerted him of an incoming threat from the vicinity of the Mudaysis Airbase.

No surprises there, Graeter thought.

After all, Air Force intelligence knew that the Iraqis had forward-deployed their MiG-23s and French-built Mirage F1 fighters to the area. Thus, Graeter and his *Citgo* comrades expected some of these bandits to take flight.

Simultaneous with the AWACS alert, however, Graeter noticed a blip on his own radar screen—"about 22 to 25 miles off my nose heading northwest." He was certain that this was the same bandit that the AWACS had detected. Suddenly, Graeter's radar detected a second bandit in the air. Moments later, Graeter's wingman, Captain Scott Maw, called out a *third* bandit.

The Iraqis now had three planes in the air.

Returning his focus to the lead bandit, Graeter noticed the Iraqi was climbing to 5,000 feet. "He was generally heading towards the track of the F-15Es," said Graeter. "We'll never know exactly what he was doing, but my guess was that he had been scrambled on the E models. If they [Iraqis] had any kind of radar, they would have known there was aircraft in the vicinity, but what kind of information or data he had…we'll obviously never know."

Watching the bandit from his radar screen, he saw the Iraqi plane stabilize its descent at about 7,000 feet. Ramping down to intercept, Graeter jettisoned his external fuel tanks to pick up speed and identified the bandit from a distance of 10 miles. It was an

A pilot from 1st Tactical Fighter Wing is silhouetted against the sun as he climbs into the cockpit of his F–15C before a sortie during Operation Desert Shield. (US Air Force)

Iraqi Mirage F1. Of the numerous planes in Iraq's inventory, the Mirage F1 was among the only respectable fighters. A French export, the F1 variants had found their way into the service of several Gulf State air forces. The Kuwaitis, Qataris, Jordanians, and even the Libyans had made extensive use of the Mirage fighter. During the Iran-Iraq War, Iranian F-14 pilots remembered that the Mirage F1 was the only Iraqi fighter that could truly hold its own in a dogfight. Today, however, this Iraqi Mirage would fall victim to Graeter's missile.

Locking onto the Mirage, Graeter fired off his AIM-7. "Even though in academics we had always discussed not looking at the missile when you shoot to preserve your night vision, I looked." Thankfully, the flash didn't impact Graeter's night vision enough to prevent him witnessing the "bright, yellow conical blast as the missile detonated." The blast, he recalled, "looked just like a cone because of the airspeed of the missile taking the flame forward. The eerie part of all of this is that there is no noise…so you get all this in visual only. It lit up the ground below and the cloud deck above, so it had an eerie look to it."

Moments later, Graeter witnessed a secondary explosion on the ground in the vicinity of the Mirage wreckage. Just as before, this explosion illuminated the ground below and the cloud cover above. Looking at the explosion, Graeter could tell that it was the wreckage of another Mirage F1.

Graeter was confused.

Neither he nor his wingman had shot down the second Mirage. How then, had the enemy bandit crashed?

Back at the airbase, the unit's Chief of Intelligence confirmed that both offending aircraft had indeed been Mirage F1s, and that the Iraqi Air Command had scrambled both in response to the F-15E strike packages. Later, it was determined that the second Mirage had crashed while reacting defensively to Graeter's killing of the first Mirage. Essentially, the second Mirage pilot had been spooked after seeing his wingman killed, and subsequently crashed his own plane in a panic. Thus, Graeter was credited with *two* Mirage kills for January 17, 1991.

Elsewhere in Iraq, Captain Steve Tate, from the 71st Fighter Squadron, was pursuing his own Mirage F1. Two weeks prior, he had been tasked to be the mission commander for the first strike package into Baghdad. "We were tasked to do a pre-strike sweep escort mission for a squadron of F-4G Wild Weasels, a squadron of F-111s, EF-111s, F-15Es, and B-52s."

Taking flight over Baghdad, Tate switched the plane's Master Arm to "On"—activating every missile and gun tube aboard his F-15. "It was a beautiful moonlit night," he recalled. "The fires in Kuwait were still burning off to the east, and the Tigris and Euphrates Rivers were easily discernable with lights. Baghdad seemed like a peaceful city until we were about 80 miles south…when the F-117s dropped their bombs."

At that moment, the skies over Baghdad erupted with anti-aircraft fire.

Tate took pause to marvel at the incoming streams of red and white anti-aircraft tracers illuminating the nighttime sky. "It was certainly the best Fourth of July fireworks display I will ever see."

Returning his attention to the enemy airspace, Tate picked up the radar signature of an incoming bogey—30 miles out and closing in fast. "We immediately jettisoned our external fuel tanks and started interrogating the contact to determine friend or foe." It turned out to be a flight of F-111s—"who were very early for their time on target." After identifying them as friendly, Tate and his wingmen vectored back onto their previous flight pattern.

Suddenly, as he was approaching Baghdad, Tate's radar alerted him to another incoming bogey, this time at 8,000 feet and 16 miles to his front. The nearby AWACS, however, had not identified the bogey on their own screens. Was this 'bogey' another friendly aircraft on egress? Within moments, however, Tate confirmed that the mysterious aircraft was a Mirage F1—"the Iraqis' frontline fighter."

From a distance of 12 miles, Tate fired his first AIM-7 Sparrow.

"Fox 1 on an F-1," he bellowed—indicating he had fired the first of his Sparrows.

At the same time, however, the Iraqi missile sites began launching a fusillade of SAMs in Tate's direction.

Before taking evasive action, Tate radioed the F-4G Wild Weasel commander, alerting him that he had fired a Sparrow at the incoming Mirage. But the Wild Weasal commander promptly radioed back that his flight group had fired their HARM missiles at the incoming SAMs—diverting the missiles' flight patterns or otherwise knocking them from the sky before they could reach Tate's position.

"What teamwork!" Tate beamed.

Adding to the exuberance was the fact that Tate's missile had killed the Iraqi Mirage. As he recalls, "the AIM-7 impacted the F1 in the left wing root. It was a huge fireball that illuminated the entire jet." The F1's fiery carcass dissolved into several more pieces

Captain Cesar Rodriguez and one of his maintenance crewmen conduct their final preparations before a combat mission, January 1991. As a member of the 58th Fighter Squadron, Rodriguez shot down two Iraqi planes during Desert Storm—a MiG-23 and a MiG-29. Eight years later, during the air war over Yugoslavia, Rodriguez shot down a Serbian MiG-29 near the city of Pristina. (US Air Force)

Ground crewmen move a weapons skid after securing an external fuel tank to an F–15C prior to its takeoff during Operation Desert Storm. (US Air Force)

of debris as it plummeted into the ground.

"Splash on the F1!" he called into the radio.

Later—during the daylight hours of January 17, 1991—one of Graeter's and Kelk's wingmen in the 58th, Captain Charles Magill (callsign: "Sly"), became the first Marine aviator to earn a confirmed kill since Vietnam. Magill was an "exchange pilot" from the Marine Corps who had been temporarily assigned to the 58th Tactical Fighter Squadron in the fall of 1989. By the time of his arrival, Magill had already logged about 1,200 hours aboard the F/A-18 Hornet. Settling into his new "broadening assignment," he had become quite adept at piloting the F-15 Eagle.

As Kelk and Graeter returned from their nighttime missions, Magill recalled: "I'll never forget the looks on their faces. They had all been shot at a bunch. They were tired, emotional, and pretty excited. I was envious, since they were now 'seasoned' combat pilots, and had the first real combat missions under their belts, and even a couple of kills."

"I started our briefing around 10:00 AM, and besides our eight guys [the second iteration of the *Citgo* and *Pennzoil* flight groups], the wing commander and a bunch of other folks were there. When Intel started briefing the enemy air defense picture—the heavily-defended target area to include the missile engagement zones—I looked over at my wingman, and his eyes were the size of silver dollars. I think I went through two bottles of water during that brief, my mouth was so dry." Magill had never been this nervous before, and he could deduce that his wingman felt likewise. Nevertheless, Magill told him that as long as they watched each other's backs, they'd be fine. Climbing aboard his F-15, Magill recalled that the moment he ignited his engine, "all the nerves left. I just

Col. Rick N. Parsons

Colonel Rick Parsons, commander of the 33d Tactical Fighter Wing, prepares his plane for combat. As a wing commander, Parsons flew several combat sorties over Iraq, where he was credited with multiple air-to-air victories. (US Air Force)

focused on the mission."

Launching with the second iteration of the *Citgo* flight, Magill went airborne with eight other F-15s that morning. With *Citgo* taking the lead, their sister formation, *Pennzoil*, occupied the right flank of their combined formation. Almost immediately, the nearby AWACS alerted them of two incoming bogeys from the south.

Both were identified as MiG-29s.

As *Citgo* and *Pennzoil*, continued pushing northward, it appeared that the MiGs were travelling in a north–south formation, at a low altitude. "We can see the bandits on our radars," said Magill, "and we sample them occasionally." As Magill's *Citgo* formation was targeting this group of MiGs, Captain Rick Tollini (callsign: "Kluso"), who was leading *Pennzoil*, asked to break away from the combined flight group to reconnoiter the Al Assad airbase a few miles northward. "It was important to monitor Al Assad," Magill said, "as it had over 70 fighters there, and it had not been hit the first night." Indeed, between the Al Taqqadum and Al Assad air bases had more than 100 Iraqi fighters. MiGs from both bases had flown sorties during the first night of the air campaign, and Magill fully expected them to "launch the fleet" at the incoming F-15s. "They could have made it very interesting for us," he recalled, "even with eight Eagles." After some brief consideration, Magill agreed to let Tollini inspect Al Assad.

Moments later, however, Magill's radar erupted with the sound of incoming SAMs— "SA-2 and SA-3 SAMs targeting me." Magill started scanning the horizon for the telltale smoke trails, but saw that the sky was clear. But suddenly, one of Magill's wingmen, Captain Tony Schiavi (callsign: "Kimo") called out "Smoke in the air!"—indicating that the SAMs were now visible.

Jumping into survival mode, Magill ordered the *Citgo* formation to jettison their external fuel tanks. Releasing their tanks as they arced into their dive, one of Magill's wingmen recalled that one of the most mesmerizing things he had ever seen was "the eight tanks coming off in perfect unison while we broke away and down." Magill and his comrades dove for 15,000 feet, picking up speed as they evaded the incoming SAMs. As it turned out, *Citgo* had stumbled across an Iraqi ground unit—"and all they had to do to see us was look up, so they targeted us. I'm not sure how many missiles were shot, since I never saw them." Magill later recalled that, up to this point, everything about the mission had seemed sterile—"just like another training mission"—until his Master Alarm went off. "That really got my attention," he said. "This wasn't a training mission, and they're trying to kill us! That's when the intensity really ramped up. I've got a lot of speed now, and the Eagle cockpit is loud like a freight train, the radios are going off…and we're only 30 miles from a merge with one of the best enemy fighters in the world."

After evading the SAMs, Magill radioed the AWACS, asking them to confirm the bearing and range to the MiG-29. Turning his formation onto a 30-degree heading, Magill soon detected the bandits at 30 miles out. "As we get into 22 miles," he recalled, "the bandits turned cold," meaning that they were turning away from the F–15s and heading northward. "I'm thinking: This is it," said Magill. "They [the MiGs] are going to land, launch the fleet at us, open up all the SAM sites and shred us—but they don't."

Thus, Magill decided to run the bandits down.

"We all go to full afterburner and accelerate out." Closing within 16 miles, the bandits suddenly turned back to meet the F–15s head on—accelerating to 600 knots.

At fourteen miles, one of Magill's wingmen, Captain Rhory Draeger (callsign: "Hoser") got radar lock on one of the MiGs—firing a single AIM-7.

Ground-guide personnel walk alongside an F-15C from the 1st Tactical Fighter Wing as the aircraft taxis across the apron during Operation Desert Shield. (US Air Force)

An F-15D Eagle sits in a revetment in Saudi Arabia. Four Patriot surface-to-air missile launchers are visible in the background. (US Air Force)

"Fox 1!" Draeger cried.

The Sparrow missile found its mark on one of the bandits, striking the MiG right through its canopy. Magill, meanwhile, set his own radar lock onto the second MiG—"showing about 1,250 knots closure." From a distance of 12 miles, Magill fired his own AIM-7. "I'd shot a lot of 2.75 folding fin rockets in the [F-18] Hornet, and sometimes the fins don't work, and they go off like bottle rockets, going crazy. I had also shot a lot of AIM-7s, but this one came off and went straight for the ground." Not impressed by the AIM-7's wild trajectory, Magill lined up another shot and fired his second Sparrow of the day. "I had read a lot of Vietnam reports, and many guys had reported time compression during the stress of combat." In other words, time itself appeared to slow down during the heat of battle. "Well," said Magill, "this is where I experienced it firsthand. As the second missile came off, everything went silent. The missile appeared to be in slow motion. I could see the yellow and brown band, the slow roll as it went out slowly. Then, at about 10 seconds time to go on the second shot, it was like someone turned all the volumes back up."

As it turned out, Magill's first missile—the missile with the seemingly errant trajectory—corrected itself and impacted the second MiG just below the right wing. As the MiG started to lurch downward, Magill's second missile—the one he had purportedly seen in slow motion—went right through the middle of the MiG-29's fuselage. "The explosion wasn't as big as I would have expected," he recalled, "just more of a sparkle and a flash."

Clearing the area, Magill called to the nearby AWACS: "Splash 2! Splash 2!"—indicating that both MiGs had been destroyed. The euphoria was short-lived, however, as Magill's radar soon lit up with warnings of more incoming SAMs. "We were right in the middle of the Baghdad MEZ [missile engagement zone]." Looking out from his canopy, Magill could see the boosters and smoke trails from the incoming SA-2, SA-3, and SA-6 missiles.

Breaking off in an evasive maneuver, Magill jettisoned his centerline fuel tank and expended the rest of his chaff, hoping to confuse the missiles as they ascended into the sky. "I saw three of them," Magill said, "but there were probably more; it was hard to count them, since they were all stacked on top of each other." But however many SAMs there may have been, Magill and his comrades successfully evaded them and returned safely to the Tabuk Air Base.

By the end of Desert Storm, Magill had logged more than 250 combat hours aboard the F-15. After the war, Magill gave several presentations at the US Navy's Fighter Weapons School—the world-renowned "Top Gun." During one of the Top Gun briefings, Magill discovered why the Iraqi MiGs had suddenly turned back towards the F-15s after previously withdrawing to the north. The MiGs had actually been trying to chase down a flight of Navy F-14s that were coming out of western Iraq. These prowling MiGs, however, had run right into Magill and his comrades in the *Citgo* flight. "Turns out that the F-14s had the MiGs about nine miles behind them, and were about to turn back into them when they saw us go over the top, shooting missiles. We never saw the Tomcats!"

Two days later—January 19, 1991—Captain Cesar Rodriguez (callsign: "Rico") achieved the first of his two kills in Desert Storm. As a member of the 58th Fighter Squadron, he had been flying alongside Jon Kelk, Rob Graeter, and Charles Magill since their deployment to the Persian Gulf. "At the end of the entire deployment," he recalled, "we had flown more than 15,000 hours, which equals two years of the peacetime flying hour program as authorized by Tactical Air Command." Rodriguez proudly recalled that his squadron "attained 16 MiG kills, the highest of any squadron during that operation. Not only did we have 16 kills, but we had the first, second, and third kills of the war. The 58th flew more sorties than any other F-15C squadron in theater, and we also had more pilots with multiple kills. There were four of us."—including Rodriguez. "What's more," he added, "during those 6,900 hours of combat operations, our maintainers produced a 98% Fully Mission Capable rate. That's unheard of in peacetime, it is unheard of in combat, and they made it look easy."

On this morning of January 19, Rodriguez would score the first of his two kills for Operation Desert Storm. As the flight leader of a four-plane formation that morning, Rodriguez and his wingmen received an alert from the nearby AWACS. As it turned out, the new intelligence data necessitated Rodriguez and his fellow pilots to redirect their focus onto several of the nearby airfields—including H-2, H-3, Mudaysis, Al-Asad, and Al-Taqqadum. "These were the main areas where we knew the Iraqis had fighters."

After an in-flight refueling, Rodriguez turned his attention back to the AWACS radio frequency. The radio traffic was definitely cluttered—fielding calls from F-16 Fighting Falcon and F-4G Wild Weasel units that were ready to initiate their bombing runs. "The new mission," Rodriguez recalled, "was a pop-up tasking to strike a newly-discovered weapons storage area southwest of Baghdad. The plan was to put 20-30 F-16s onto this target." According to the AWACS, four F-15s were to fly in front of the strike formation,

A Kuwaiti A-4 Skyhawk and an American F-15 from the 1st Tactical Fighter Wing stand on an airfield prior to a mission on February 2, 1991. Note the inscription "Free Kuwait" on the A-4's fuselage—indicating that the A-4 was part of the Kuwaiti military operating in exile. (US Air Force)

while Rodriguez and his wingman, Captain Craig Underhill (callsign: "Mole") would fly behind the formation as a "post-strike sweep" to conduct battle damage assessments and engage any MiGs that might be lingering over the target area.

"So as we arrived on the scene," he said, "everything was looking good." Indeed, the four F-15s in front of the strike group "encountered a variety of targets"—all of which were promptly engaged by the ground-attack F-16s.

But suddenly, the AWACS broke in with an urgent call.

"*Citgo* 25, pop-up contacts, 40 north of the target area."

Rodriguez had been expecting this. The AWACS call indicated that two unknown aircraft, likely enemy, had been detected approximately forty miles north. "Sure enough, at about 60 miles from us, we picked up two unidentified targets," said Rodriguez. "We were up at 30,000 feet, and we proceeded northeast as we were watching the [F-16s] attacking the target." As Rodriguez and Underhill vectored to the northeast, both pilots saw the F-16 formation heading south—thus confirming that the F-16s had delivered their strike package.

Just then, however, the trailing F-16 pilot radioed that he fallen under radar lock from one of the two unidentified aircraft coming from the north. "At this point," Rodriguez said, "we weren't sure what kind of aircraft they were, but they were about 35 miles in trail with the F-16s." The F-16s, however, weren't fazed or even threatened by the lock-on, and collectively sped southward out of the target area—just in time for Rodriguez and Underhill to intercept.

But once their F-15s were within eighteen nautical miles of the incoming bandits,

Rodriguez and Underhill were shocked to see both Iraqi planes reverse their course and retreat to the northeast—"back to their base of origin," Rodriguez surmised.

But neither he nor Underhill wanted to let these bandits live to fly another day.

After confirming from the AWACS that there were no other friendly jets in the area, Rodriguez and Underhill gave chase to the fleeting bandits. Around this time, both men confirmed that the elusive jets were MiG-29s. "They were quickly moving out of our ability to engage them, as we were in a tail-chase. They were about 12-14 miles off our nose and they had taken it down pretty low; they had pushed it up just about as fast as a MiG-29 could run." Ironically, the F-15s did not have to expend as much energy to keep up with these Iraqi MiGs. Although Rodriguez and Underhill were in pursuit at well beyond Mach 1, they did not have to send their engines to full-throttle in order to keep pace with the MiG-29. Even though these latter-day MiGs were supposedly the pride of the Eastern Bloc air forces, they were still overmatched when pitted against the F-15 Eagle.

While closing in on the Iraqi MiGs, Rodriguez and Underhill realized that they were quickly approaching Baghdad airspace. Within moments, their radar warning systems began sounding the alert of incoming SAMs. They were ready to clear the airspace when the AWACS interrupted, saying: "Citgo, pop-up targets 330 for 13"—indicating that the bandits were 13 miles away on a heading of 330 degrees. "Out of instinct," said Rodriguez, "I threw my radar into AUTOGUNS and slammed the throttles to full afterburner. I pulled 9-9.5 g's in the turn to put 330 on my nose, and at the same time, reached down and jettisoned my fuel tanks." Underhill followed suit and, within moments, both F-15s gained visual contact of the lead MiG-29.

"At this point, that MiG-29 locks me up,"—Rodriguez's radar system indicated as much. "I execute a defensive maneuver…and dispense a bunch of chaff to break his lock, and cause problems for the MiG-29's radar." Meanwhile, Underhill sprang into action against the leading MiG. Locking onto the leader, Underhill fired an AIM-7.

"Fox 1!" he cried.

Watching the missile glide off Underhill's wing, Rodriguez watched intently as the missile impacted squarely on its nose, sending the Iraqi bandit into a brilliant flash of molten steel—"literally leaving nothing," said Rodriguez, "and I mean nothing to the imagination other than a big fireball, followed by a large sparkler-like cloud as it descended to the ground."

Elated, Rodriguez called "Splash one!" to the AWACS—indicating that Underhill had just destroyed one enemy bandit. But this was no time to celebrate. For moments after the AWACS confirmed Rodriguez's report, they issued another warning:

"Second bandit, three miles in trail!"

By this point, Rodriguez and Underhill were both at a low altitude, about two and a half miles apart, and the incoming bandit was closing fast to their six o'clock position. Both F-15s executed a hard-right turn to meet the incoming bandit head-on.

But identifying this bandit would be a bit more problematic. Underhill locked onto the bandit with his radar but couldn't conclusively identify whether this radar signature was friendly or hostile. In the fast-paced, rough-and-tumble world of combat aviation, a fighter pilot has mere seconds to identify an aircraft as "friendly" or "hostile." The pilot must make positive identification—for once he fires that missile, he can never take it back. The ever-present risk of fratricide pressured every pilot to err on the side of caution if he could not identify the bogey from beyond visual range.

Today, as neither Rodriguez nor Underhill could identify the bandit using their onboard instrumentation, both continued flying forward to visually identify the incoming aircraft. "As the bandit was approaching, we attempt to identify this aircraft from the front aspect…the silhouette and plan form look a lot like our western fighters, so before we lose an opportunity to maintain an offensive position, I direct the formation to bracket. This set up the VID [visual identification] intercept, which put me in position to run directly on the threat, to get as close as I can to him and try to identify this particular threat. At about a mile and a half, and well below him, I put the bandit on my nose, and I push it up to five stages of burner. As I pass below his left wing by 50-100 feet, I can clearly see the Iraqi paint scheme, his national markings, and that is definitely a MiG-29. I call 'Bandit, Bandit, Bandit.'"

As Rodriguez pulled behind the MiG, its pilot began pulling a slow left turn— seemingly unaware that an American F-15 was moving in behind him. At some point, however, the Iraqi pilot was alerted to Rodriguez's presence, because the MiG soon started to accelerate and vector into a defensive turn.

Closing in to about 3,000 feet, Rodriguez brought the nose of his aircraft up to align an AIM-7 missile shot. "I opt to go with the AIM-7," he said, "as we are at a low altitude over the hot desert, and we had seen some problems with the heatseeking AIM-9 [Sidewinder] in this environment." This phenomenon had been a recurring problem with the heatseeking missile. Although heatseeking missiles were a tremendous asset in a dogfight, a pilot had to be careful in how he employed them. As the name implied, the missile would lock on to a target by following the heat from its exhaust manifold. However, the heat-seeking apparatus could easily be fooled by other nearby heat signatures. For instance, if a pilot fired his AIM-9 in the direction of a rising or setting sun, the missile would track onto the sun, and burn out as it chased the solar heat. Likewise, if a pilot fired a heatseeking missile while flying close to the ground (especially a hot desert floor) the missile would nose-dive towards the ground-level heat. Thus, for today's confrontation, Rodriguez selected his radar-tracked AIM-7 Sparrow.

Meanwhile, the Iraqi MiG, perhaps in a state of panic, tried to shake Rodriguez by performing a "Split-S" maneuver. According to Rodriguez, the Split-S was a defensive action wherein an enemy plane rolls upside down, pulls downward, and reverses course— usually as a means to disengage from combat. Rodriguez, however, "wasn't going to take any chances," he said. "So I rolled hard off his tail and climbed it up to the vertical. I then rolled to look down and reacquire a tally on the bandit. I then witness the bandit impact the ground." Indeed, while attempting to evade Rodriguez, the Iraqi pilot had inadvertently plummeted himself into the ground. "As he hit the desert floor," Rodriguez continued, "he hadn't quite gotten perpendicular to the ground. I could clearly see his afterburners cooking, and his stabs were dug in…and the wreckage continues to create a fireball for miles across the desert."

Reflecting on the engagement, Rodriguez commented that "through hard training and solid squadron standards between flight leads and wingmen, Mole [Underhill] and I were able to successfully complete this piece of the mission, with surprisingly little comm. We knew what each of us was doing."

Returning from its mission, an American F-15 returns to its revetment in Saudi Arabia. (US Air Force)

Cesar Rodriguez achieved his second kill of Desert Storm a few days later, on January 26, 1991—this time against a MiG-23. Among the Soviet-built fighters, the MiG-23 and its variants were among the most derided. Although its "swing wing" design was revolutionary for the time, the aircraft was an exceptionally poor dogfighter. The Israeli and Iranian pilots whom had flown against the MiG-23 were unanimous in their disdain for it. As one US Marine pilot recalled: "The MiG-23 was a maneuvering 'dog.' Even the F-4 Phantom could out-turn it." Thus, it came as no surprise that the MiG-23 was easy prey for coalition fighters.

By January 26, barely one week into the air campaign, Saddam was already against the ropes. Several air-defense sites had been destroyed, along with several more Command & Control nodes. At airbases across Iraq, much of Saddam's air force was destroyed before it even got off the ground. Meanwhile, the "Butcher of Baghdad" began firing Scud missiles into Israel, hoping to bring the Israelis into the conflict, and fracture the coalition along religious lines. Although the Scuds were a persistent nuisance, they were notoriously inaccurate and often landed harmlessly in the desert or into the Mediterranean Sea. Very often, they were intercepted by American Patriot missiles in mid-flight. In fact, General H. Norman Schwarzkopf, the commander of UN forces in the Gulf, once quipped that he was more afraid of being struck by lightning than being hit by a Scud missile.

On this morning of January 26, as the Iraqi Air Force was struggling to survive, Cesar Rodriguez was more concerned about the weather. Poor weather conditions had already grounded much of the coalition's aircraft. Of the few aircraft that did take flight that day, most were "Defensive Counter Air" missions—in this case, roaming air patrols looking for any opportunistic targets and keeping the airspace clear for friendly recon flights.

An F-15E Strike Eagle taxiing down the flight line. By 1990, the Strike Eagle community was relatively new and many of its pilots had been drawn from other units, namely F-4 Phantom squadrons that were phasing out the latter. During Desert Storm, the F-15E Strike Eagle units engaged mostly ground targets. There was only one recorded air-to-air kill for the Strike Eagle variant during the Gulf War. (US Air Force)

Taking flight as part of a four-plane formation, Rodriguez was manning the Number 3 position. The flight leader for this mission was Captain Rhory Draeger, who himself had gotten a MiG kill earlier that week. Draeger's wingman was Captain Tony Schiavi. Rodriguez's wingman was Captain Bruce Till. Rodriguez's normal wingman, Craig Underhill, was back at the airbase, completing his turn for the rotational "squadron supervisor" position.

Although the war was now into its second week, today's sortie had been relatively uneventful. The local AWACS had called in a few contact reports—most of which turned out to be false alarms. Rodriguez and his wingmen continued lumbering forward along their flight path until the AWACS interrupted once again. This time, the controller reported aircraft activity near the H-2 and H-3 airfields farther west.

Acknowledging the call, the formation headed southwest, maintaining their altitude above 30,000 feet so as to conserve fuel and stat above the cloud deck. "At about 80 miles," recalled Rodriguez, "AWACS informs us that there are aircraft taking off, and as we approached 70 miles, we also get radar contact. Thanks to some fantastic support from the AWACS, we were informed that these were MiG-23s before we even had a chance to lock up the contacts." As the formation proceeded to merge with the incoming MiGs, Rodriguez noticed that, based on his map, these MiGs appeared to be following a major highway northeast towards Baghdad. "Our post-flight speculation," he said, "was that once these aircraft landed, they would refuel and attempt to run to Iran." Indeed, this second week of the air campaign marked the beginning of the mass exodus of Iraqi aircraft to Iran. Wanting to preserve what was left of their air force, several Iraqi units began flying jets into Iran, hoping to use the shield of Iranian neutrality as a means to wait out the conflict.

"The clouds were still pretty thick," Rodriguez continued. "So we didn't think that we were going to see the missiles do their job, but at forty miles the clouds started to break, and we could see all the way to the ground." This was fortuitous, as the F-15s could now identify the MiG-23 visually, without the use of instrumentation. "Rhory collapsed the formation so we could get through a hole in the clouds in our descent. Once underneath, at about 15,000 feet he spread the formation back out into the wall, and that's when the enemy formation became clear. The MiG-23s were in a 'Vic' formation [Flying-V], with the leader on the point, and the two wingmen space aft on a 45-degree line on each side. There was a two-mile space between the leader and the other two as they navigated along the highway."

Accelerating to merge with the MiGs, Draeger went after the leader, Schiavi went after the northern arm, while Till and Rodriguez targeted the southern arm. Draeger fired first, launching an AIM-7 into the lead MiG. Although the missile catapulted squarely into the MiGs fuselage, it surprisingly did not detonate. Instead, the missile ripped through the intake manifold, shattering the MiG's engine. The ailing bandit careened to its left before the shattered engine caught fire, engulfing the pilot in flames.

Till and Rodriguez, meanwhile, fired their AIM-7 missiles almost simultaneously at the third, southernmost MiG. Luckily for Rodriguez, his missile landed first—sending the MiG hurtling into the desert floor and confirming his second kill of the Gulf War. Draeger and Shiavi, meanwhile, made short order of the other two MiGs. "None of the MiG pilots managed to eject," said Rodriguez.

Rodriguez later recalled that he and Draeger were the only two pilots in that formation who had previous MiG kills. Schiavi and Till had yet to engage any MiGs and wondered how Rodriguez and Draeger could have remained so calm during the engagement. "The prior experience helped us stay calm," he admitted, "and our wingmen perceived this, and it helped them execute very well in their first engagement." By the end of the conflict, American F-15s had downed at least five additional MiG-23s.

On February 2, 1991, an American F-15 achieved another milestone by downing an Iraqi Ilyushin Il-76. Unlike the MiGs and Mirages that had thus far fallen prey to American fighters, the Il-76 was a general-purpose airlift plane. It was the first confirmed kill of a non-fighter aircraft by an F-15. Scoring the kill was Captain Greg Masters (callsign: "Dutch") of the 525th Fighter Squadron—the famous "Bulldogs."

On the 2d of February, Masters recalled: "I was an air-to-air mission commander, and had eight F-15s and four F-16s at my disposal to protect a large F-16 striking force attacking an airfield south of Kirkuk, as well as other High Value Airborne Assets (HVAAs) north of the border, and to cutoff Iraqi aircraft attempting to escape into Iran." Masters's patrol was flying east of Kirkuk, near the Iranian border when his wingman got a radar contact at 4,000 feet. "We chased him down as he headed west to Kirkuk," said Masters. "We were five miles behind him and closing fast by the time I ascertained he was not a friendly and shot my first AIM-7 Sparrow." Masters jettisoned his fuel tank and prepared to follow-up with another missile shot, but the first missile, as he said, "glided perfectly."

Because of the heavy cloud cover, neither Masters nor his wingmen could see the explosion. They were certain, nonetheless, that it had been a kill. However, Masters and his flight group were getting dangerously close to the SAM missile batteries in Kirkuk— "so I was more interested in keeping my wingmen out of trouble than celebrating a victory or confirming the kill. It was a long mission, so by the time I got back on the ground I had forgotten about the engagement." For the maintenance handlers, however, the sight of the missing AIM-7 gave them cause to start painting an Iraqi flag on the side of Masters's plane. "I hated to rain on their parade," he said, "but since the impact occurred below the clouds, we couldn't confirm the kill at that time."

The kill was confirmed later, however, as an Il-76. The media reported that this Il-76 may have been the same plane that was carrying the Iraqi Air Marshal back from Iran, where he had been coordinating the delivery and placement of Iraqi fighters fleeing into Persia.

Meanwhile, back in the 58th Fighter Squadron, pilots like Captain Tony Murphy (callsign: ET) continued patrolling the skies of eastern Iraq—on the lookout for any opportunistic targets. On February 7, 1991, Captain Murphy—still untested in combat—scored his first aerial kills, downing two Iraqi Su-22 fighter-bombers.

To this point, the 58th had flown more than twenty combat sorties since the opening volleys of Desert Storm—"and the only engagement I had been involved with," said Murphy, "was back in December [1990]." During that sortie, Murphy and his wingman were flying along the Saudi border when three Iraqi jets populated on the F-15s' radar. These jets collectively took turns "charging the border"—but after fifteen minutes of playing cat-and-mouse, the Iraqi fighters broke away and returned to their base. "That was the closest action I had seen prior to the shootdown. His comrades in the 58th— including Kelk, Graeter, Rodriguez, and Magill—had all scored kills, and Murphy was eager to claim one of his own.

By February 7, the 58th Fighter Squadron had been patrolling along the Iranian border. Because Murphy's regular wingman had to return to the States early, the squadron had rendered Murphy a "pick-up pilot" of sorts—filling in for other pilots and missions as needed. On this day, the commander of the 33d Tactical Fighter Wing, Colonel Rick Parsons, was leading the sortie. Thus, Murphy was tasked to be his wingman.

Until now, most of the sorties had been four-plane formations but because this had been a short-alert tasking, it was only Parsons and Murphy who were going aloft. Such pairings between a junior and senior officer were not uncommon. "We had flown together occasionally," said Murphy, "so this was not our first sortie together."

The briefing and launch were uneventful, "and we proceeded due east to bootleg a tanker that had a little extra gas," said Murphy. "From there, we wanted to go due north on the east side of Baghdad to avoid all the SAM sites around the city. Our standard load-out was three bags of gas and four each of AIM-7s and AIM-9s, plus the gun. Our plan was to get past the SAMs and patrol in a north-south pattern, versus the usual east-west. We had just passed north of Baghdad when my wingman called out a radar contact. I moved my radar up and saw the same. AWACS confirmed that were we the

Captain Tony Murphy, of the 58th Fighter Squadron, returns to base after downing two Iraqi Su-22 fighter-bombers, February 1991. (US Air Force)

An F-15E Strike Eagle displays its GBU-28 precision-guided bombs. During Desert Storm, attack aircraft like the F-15E Strike Eagle and the F-117 Nighthawk made extensive use of laser-guided and optically-guided missiles to engage targets. The GBU-28 was a 5,000-pound bomb designated for "bunker busting"—i.e. destroying heavily-fortified troop positions. (US Air Force)

only friendly aircraft in the area, so it was starting to firm up in my mind that these were hostile groups."

Murphy started the intercept by vectoring east, targeting the group leader. After verifying that the target was in range, Murphy locked onto the bandit and fired an AIM-7. "My missile comes off and appears to be tracking to the target." As Murphy brought up the nose of his aircraft to center the bandit on his Heads-Up Display, he suddenly noticed a bright flash and the sight of the Su-22 rolling in the dirt.

Setting his sights onto the second bandit in the formation, Murphy quickly locked onto the Su-22 and fired his second AIM-7. "Right then," he recalled, "the AWACS calls that the border is 15 miles on our nose"—meaning that Murphy was only a few moments away from violating Iranian airspace. Murphy jinked his F-15 southward to put more airspace between himself and the border—just in time to see his second missile lose its lock on the bandit. Undeterred, Murphy fired another AIM-7, downing the second Su-22 with a solid hit just behind the canopy. "This is when I realize two things," he said. "First, is that the distance from his aircraft to his shadow was the same as his wingspan! So he's about 50 feet [in altitude]. Second, this is the first time I realize that I'm at only 100 feet! It shows you how focused you can get on the target."

Although he was certain that his target was a Sukhoi Su-22, or even an early-generation MiG, it was not until later that Air Intelligence confirmed his kills to be Su-22s. The Su-22 had been a frequent visitor to American air patrols in and around the Middle East. In 1981, for example, two Libyan Su-22s had engaged a pair of F-14 Tomcats over the Gulf of Sidra. Both Sukhois were promptly destroyed by the American Tomcats. Today's brief dogfight had been no different. Both Su-22s plummeted to the Earth—victims of the AIM-7 missile.

As Murphy pulled up from the engagement, he spied another Iraqi aircraft in flames, hurtling towards the ground. Murphy's wingman, Colonel Parsons, had just downed a Sukhoi Su-7—another fighter of similar vintage to the MiG-21. Back at the Tabuk Air Base, Murphy and Parsons were met by a reporter from *Airman Magazine*. "I filed a claim that day for two kills," said Murphy, "and confirmed Colonel Parsons's kill."

Four days later, in the 525th Fighter Squadron, Captains Steve Dingee and Mark Mackenzie had the unique honor of "sharing" credit for killing an enemy aircraft. It was the first time a shared kill had been registered since Vietnam. Between January 19 and February 11, 1991, Dingee, Mackenzie, and their wingmen had flown dozens of sorties. At first, their missions focused on Combat Air Patrols and providing cover for attack missions. By mid-February, however, the missions were changing.

"We had destroyed the Iraqi Air Force, in the air and on the ground," he said. "They then decided that, to save their air force, they would fly to Iran. So we started flying CAPs [Combat Air Patrols] along the Iranian border 24 hours a day to keep the Iraqis from being able to get out of the country. Numerous aircraft were destroyed along the way. It was on one of these missions that we stumbled across a helicopter. Helicopters were not a big threat to us in the air, and not worth engaging if there was something else going on. But if we detected one on the way home, we would definitely divert some assets to go take care of it."

That day was the first and only time Dingee flew with Mackenzie, as the former's regular wingman was sick. While returning from their aerial border patrol as part of a six-plane formation, Dingee detected some helicopter traffic on his radar. By its location, he could tell it was the same helicopter activity he had detected earlier. Confirming from the AWACS that there were no friendly helicopters in the area, Dingee and Mackenzie vectored to intercept the enemy chopper, which turned out to be an Iraqi Mi-8.

"We dropped down to about 12-13,000 [feet]," Dingee said, "but wouldn't go any lower because AAA and SAMs became more of threat at lower altitudes." From a distance of nearly seven nautical miles, Dingee and Mackenzie almost simultaneously fired their AIM-7s at the Iraqi helicopter. "It was an awesome sight to see the smoke trails converge on the target. The aircraft just fell out of the sky after my missile fused near him. There was not a big explosion and fireball like the Mirage F-1s. It hit the ground, and there was a plume of black smoke and dust from where it hit, probably 8-10 seconds after my missile detonated."

Throughout the air war, American pilots downed at least five additional helicopters—one of which was scored by an F-15E Strike Eagle. It was the first and only air-to-air victory for the Strike Eagle variant of the F-15. Captain Richard Bennett and his Weapons Systems Officer (WSO), Captain Dan Bakke, were assigned to the 335th Fighter Squadron. Unlike its air-superiority counterpart, the F-15E was a standard two-seater—accommodating a pilot and a WSO who assisted with navigational duties. The F-15E was purportedly just as versatile for ground-attack missions as it was for air-to-air combat. On the afternoon of February 13, 1991, Bennett and Bakke would showcase the Strike Eagle's air-to-air capabilities as they downed an Iraqi helicopter.

As coalition forces approached the one-month anniversary of the air war, the ground-attack aviation units ran their sorties at a furious pace—engaging targets with a variety of "smart" and "dumb" bombs. But whether their bombs were laser-guided, or purely gravity-fed, these F-15Es, A-10 Thunderbolts, A-6 Intruders, and F-117 Nighthawks pounded Iraqi targets with relentless fury.

On February 13, Bennett and Bakke went aloft as part of a "benign Scud patrol." Scuds were still a nuisance and the F-15Es could zero-in on a mobile Scud launcher and destroy it if needed. "Since there wasn't a lot of Scud activity that night," said Bakke, "we were in the process of prosecuting an attack on one of our alternate target sets, an SA-3 site located halfway between Baghdad and Al-Qaim. It was not an active SAM site, as it had already been hit by the very, very capable F-4G Wild Weasels. We were attempting to hit the individual missile launchers to keep the site off the air, permanently."

Just then, however, Bennett received an urgent call from the AWACS:

"Packard 41 [Bennett's and Bakke's callsign], we have three enemy helicopters dismounting troops. Possible troops in contact. Kill all helicopters."

Bennett acknowledged the call, though he and Bakke were a little confused by it. To this point, their typical instructions had been to "identify" and "investigate." Thus, the newfound "kill" tasking was a welcomed change of pace.

As Bennett took the Strike Eagle down into its attack run, Bakke began his complex choreography at the radar instrument panel. Using the Strike Eagle's advanced LANTIRN targeting pod system, Bakke positively identified two helicopters from 50-60 miles out. Given the relative position of the two choppers, Bakke was certain that they were still on the ground delivering troops. "Our mindset was turning to a ground attack. With what we're seeing and the information from AWACS, I don't think any of us were thinking anything else."

Before engaging the helicopters, however, Bakke radioed the AWACS one more time to confirm that the target was, in fact, Iraqi.

The AWACS then repeated its earlier transmission: "Kill all helicopters."

With that, Bakke, released the GBU-10 bomb, which hurtled into the lead helicopter. After making impact, however, Bakke and Bennett saw the bomb continue its downward trajectory after ripping through the enemy's cockpit. It was then that they realized the helicopter was still *in flight*—thus rendering their kill an "air-to-air victory."

Within seconds, the helicopter "disintegrated into a huge fireball." Elated, Bakke radioed to the AWACS that he had killed the first helicopter and was preparing to engage the second. His jubilance, however, quickly turned to despair when the AWACS controller radio back:

"Packard 41, confirm you VID [visually identified] the helicopter as Iraqi."

Bakke was incredulous.

"I admittedly went into a tirade on the radio." The AWACS had been adamant about the F-15E killing these "confirmed" helicopters. Now, the AWACS had apparently second-guessed itself and was asking Bakke to visually confirm that the helicopter had truly been Iraqi and not American. "Because we no longer understood the tactical situation," said Bakke, "we could not engage the second helicopter. It was a very quiet cockpit on the way home. I don't think either of us said a word." To make matters worse, they could not rapidly identify the remains of the helicopter because a friendly strike force was in-bound to the vicinity. Thus, Bennett and Bakke had to vacate the area before they became victims of fratricide.

Chief of Staff of the Air Force, General Merrill A. McPeak, performs a pre-flight check on an F-15D Eagle during his visit to a coalition airbase in Saudi Arabia, 1991. (US Air Force)

Fortunately, after they returned to base, Bennett and Bakke were relieved to discover that the helicopter had, in fact, been Iraqi. Moreover, their destruction of the helicopter saved the lives of an American Special Forces team whom the Iraqi heliborne troops had been sent to intercept. Although Bennett's and Bakke's mission had been a success, they never forgot the AWACS's agony-inducing radio call. Nevertheless, both men flew several more missions together during Desert Storm—43 in total.

Although the F-15E had claimed its first aerial kill, the true test of its mettle came in the various ground-attack missions it flew over Iraq. At the start of the air war, the 335th and 336th Fighter Squadrons carried the day with their precision air strikes. On that first day of the air campaign, five Scud missile sites were attacked by twenty-four F-15E Strike Eagles. Typically, the F-15Es flew in formations of three to six planes.

Each Strike Eagle carried a mix of air-to-air and air-to-ground munitions. These mission stores consisted of AIM-9 missiles for aerial targets and MK20 Rockeye CBUs or Mk82 bombs for ground targets. With this heavy ordnance configuration, the F-15E was limited in how it could maneuver. Indeed, the Strike Eagle was prohibited from executing any turns beyond 3g for fear that it would damage the airframe or induce a loss of control.

On that first night of the air war, Lieutenant Steve Kwast, an F-15E pilot with the 336th, recalled his flight group's attack on a Scud missile site. Attacking these Scud platforms was sure to be risky: each site was ringed by multiple layers of air defense guns.

As they crossed into Iraqi airspace, Kwast recalled that "we could see the fires burning at the observation posts and radar facilities that our Special Forces had taken out." When

Aircraft from the 4th Fighter Wing (including two F-15Es, an F-15C, and two F-16s) fly over the burning oil wells in Kuwait, set ablaze by the retreating Iraqi Army, February 1991. (US Department of Defense)

Kwast and his wingmen approached the target area, they began to the think about their primary and alternate attack plans. Which option they chose depended on the amount of anti-aircraft fire. If it was too heavy, the strike formation would fly high. If the enemy fire were light, the Strike Eagles would fly low. Seeing the virtual "wall" of air defense fire rising from the desert floor, it came as no surprise when Kwast heard the flight leader give the order to "climb." Every F-15E in the formation climbed to a higher altitude and released its Mk82 gravity-fed "dumb" bombs. After delivering their bombs to the target, Kwast recalled seeing more than 100 anti-aircraft pieces firing at the Strike Eagles as they egressed from the target area. At the time, Kwast was the only lieutenant pilot in the 336th Fighter Squadron—most of the other flight officers were captains. He also had the distinction of being one of the so-called "baby" F-15E pilots, meaning that he had gone straight from undergraduate flight training to the F-15E familiarization course. By 1990, the Strike Eagle community was relatively new, and the Air Force was still trying to fill the ranks of its newfound "strike fighter" units. As such, the flight-hour qualifications to be an "experienced" F-15E pilot were much lower than in the established F-15A and F-15C units. For example, 200 flight hours in a new F-15E unit was enough to be an "experienced" aviator. However, in an F-15C unit like the 58th Fighter Squadron, 200 hours wasn't even enough to qualify a pilot for a back-up flight lead position.

During the daylight raids, F-15E preferred the "dive toss" technique. From 30,000 feet, the pilot would roll inverted and dive towards the aim point for final visual identification. The pilot would then pull out of the roll at about 15,000 feet, beyond the maximum reach for Iraqi air defense guns. When the pilot lined up the proper aim point, he would release his bomb to the target.

Captain Bill Schaal and Major Jerry Oney, both of whom deployed with the 336th, flew the first of their combat sorties together during the daytime. It was a nerve-racking experience, as both men preferred to attack under the cover of night. Their mission, however, turned out to be more humorous than hair-raising. On one of the major highways below, Schaal saw someone hauling a boat. "We both got a good chuckle out of that," said Oney.

During their second mission, both men were dispatched to eliminate some mobile Scud sites. A section of A-10s had been looking for these Scuds but hadn't found them before running low on fuel and needing to top off. Thus, Schaal, Oney, and their wingmen, went on the hunt for the elusive Scuds. During their patrol, Oney noticed a smaller air defense site, manned by what seemed to be a quad-barrel anti-aircraft gun. Oney wanted to drop a Mk82 on it but, as he admitted, his flight group had other priorities.

Continuing along their uneventful flight pattern, Schaal and Oney were alerted by the sudden appearance of an Iraqi SAM. Oney then saw the flight leader initiate his evasive maneuvers, turning into the direction of the SAM so as to thwart its trajectory. Oney watched in amazement as the SAM overshot the leader's position and explode about 500 feet above him. Luckily the flight leader's F-15E was unscathed. But for Schaal and Oney, this Iraqi SAM had been too close for comfort. As it were, the Scuds had been hard to find because the Iraqis had become more adept at camouflaging them—"hiding mobile Scuds in specially-adapted buses and underneath road bridges."

Although the F-15E's only aerial kill was the aforementioned helicopter, the Strike Eagle did have a few close encounters with enemy MiGs. The F-15E's disposition towards enemy MiGs depended largely on who the flight leader was for any given mission. Some strike leaders opted to avoid MiGs entirely—calling the enemy positions to the local AWACS and letting the F-15Cs take care of them. Other strike leaders adopted the attitude: "If we see a MiG, we'll try and skirt around him if he doesn't see us. But if he sees us, we'll climb and kill him." Other flight leaders were more aggressive:

"When Eagles fly, MiGs die. Period."

In their eyes, it was better to deal with the MiG on the way to a strike mission than to deal with it on the way back. On at least one occasion, an F-15E Strike Eagle from the 4th Tactical Fighter Wing engaged a MiG-29 with an AIM-9 Sidewinder. Sadly, the MiG escaped.

On January 18 and 20, the 4th Tactical Fighter Wing respectively lost its first and second F-15Es. Neither had been downed by enemy aircraft, but one had been confirmed as a SAM kill. The first F-15E, piloted by Major Donnie Holland and WSO Major Thomas Koritz had successfully delivered their bombs against a Petroleum, Oil, and Lubricant plant near Basra. After dropping their Mk82 bombs, the plane plummeted into the ground, erupting into flames that the other aircrews could clearly see. It remains unclear if Holland and Koritz were downed by a missile (the area was heavily guarded by SAMs), or if they simply crashed while rolling out of their bombing maneuver. Nevertheless, the Iraqi government returned their bodies after the war and both men had memorial services held at Seymour Johnson Air Force Base in North Carolina.

The second F-15E, downed on January 20, was piloted by Colonel David Eberly and Major Thomas Griffith. While attacking a fixed Scud site, the pilot and WSO were

The remains of an Iraqi MiG-25 after being destroyed on the ground by a 2,000-pound laser-guided bomb. During Desert Storm, a good portion of the Iraqi Air Force was destroyed before it ever went airborne. Even more Iraqi planes were destroyed during the ensuing years as the US and its NATO partners enforced the Iraqi No-Fly Zones. (US Department of Defense)

downed by an Iraqi SA-6 missile. Both men ejected and evaded capture for the next several days. Both, however, were soon captured near the Syrian border and held as POWs until their release in March 1991.

Within a few weeks, the F-15E squadrons had firmly established their battle rhythms. Sorties were flown around the clock and the target lists varied little from day to day: SAM sites, Scud launchers, and infrastructure targets were the typical fare.

Meanwhile, men like Captain Gary Klett had the dubious distinction of being an "MQ Maggot"—a term given to any new pilot who was still in the "Mission Qualification Training" (MQT) phase. In US fighter squadrons, newly-assigned pilots had to perform MQT—"a specified sequence of sorties" that had to be completed within 90 days of joining the unit. Since Klett had only joined the 336th that December (after they had already deployed to Saudi Arabia), he was still in his MQT phase. To boot, he was relatively new to the F-15E, having started on F-4 Phantoms before being selected to attend the Strike Eagle Transition Course.

Although still technically an "MQ Maggot," Klett was selected to fly his first combat sortie during the second week of the air war. It was a short-range mission: an attack on an enemy airfield. On the way to the target, Klett recalled: "I spent the whole time finding things with the radar and running through the process to designate them as targets. I wanted to make sure I didn't dork up my first attack." Flying as part of a six-plane formation, Klett noticed the Iraqi anti-aircraft fire before he even crossed the border.

Most of it was from small-caliber guns and thus couldn't reach the higher altitudes of the F-15E.

At 20 miles from the target, he could clearly see the runway. "We rolled into a 30-degree dive about five miles from the target and waited for the computer to decide to release the bombs." One advantage of flying the F-15E was that the targeting computer removed much of the guesswork from yesteryear. Dropping their Mk82 500-pound bombs, the Strike Eagles quickly egressed from the target area, with the fiery strands of anti-aircraft bullets chasing them as they ascended.

While American F-15Cs and F-15Es destroyed Iraqi targets on the ground and in the air, the Royal Saudi Air Force (RSAF) made extensive use of their own F-15s. Throughout most of the twentieth century, the Kingdom of Saud had relied on Great Britain for its aircraft imports. However, the Shah's demise in Iran left Saudi Arabia feeling "distinctly exposed" in the early 1980s.

The RSAF had wanted to purchase the F-14 Tomcat, both for its long-range capabilities and to counter "the fact that the Iranian Shah's F-14s had potentially fallen into the wrong hands." Nevertheless, the Saudis ultimately selected the F-15 Eagle along with select deliveries of the F-16 Fighting Falcon and five E-3 AWACS. By this point, however, the Saudi F-15s had seen little action, although two had been credited with downing a pair of Iranian F-4Es that violated Saudi airspace in 1984. By 1990, the RSAF operated more than sixty F-15 airframes.

On January 24, 1991, the RSAF scored its only aerial kill in Desert Storm. Captain Ayehid Salah Al-Shamrani, assigned to the No. 13 Squadron, engaged and destroyed two Iraqi Mirage F-1 fighters over the Persian Gulf. Details of the engagement remain sketchy, but it's generally accepted that Al-Shamrani was guided onto the Mirages by an American AWACS.

The pilot, however, struggled to complete his intercept.

As the AWACS talked him onto the Mirages' position, Al-Shamrani fired two AIM-9 Sidewinders at the Iraqi jets before they could vector within striking distance of US naval vessels in the Gulf.

Although the Saudi government and the Western media confirmed the kill, the circumstances surrounding the engagement raised questions in the aviation community. As one American F-15 pilot noted: "There are several very valid questions to ask about these kills. Firstly, why is the pilot of an aircraft designed to kill BVR [from beyond visual range] doing a stern conversion to visual range without firing a shot? Secondly, where was his wingman during all of this? Thirdly, he fired both missiles while they were still 'caged,' if I recall correctly." The term "caged" referred to a heatseeking missile that was still coupled to the radar when fired. Typically, firing a heat-seeker while "caged" was considered a *faux pas*.

Regardless, the RSAF spent most of Desert Storm doing what was called "Goalie CAPs"—uneventful air patrols that were purposely placed far away from the actual fighting. And while no Saudi F-15s were lost to enemy fire in Desert Storm, one Saudi pilot did defect to Sudan. On February 14, 1991, a Saudi F-15 pilot from No. 5 Squadron departed King Fahad Air Base. It was reported to the coalition's Combined Air Operations Center (CAOC) that the F-15 had crashed. The CAOC was about to launch

The fuselage of Colonel Rick Parsons's F-15C, decorated with the markings annotating his air-to-air kills in the skies over Iraq. (US Air Force)

a search-and-rescue mission, when a CIA operative monitoring the Khartoum Airport called in and asked:

"What's this Saudi F-15 doing on the runway here?"

The aircraft was later returned to Saudi Arabia—the pilot stating that he had defected because he "could not fight against his Muslim brothers."

As the air campaign lumbered into its second month, coalition ground forces began their assault into Iraq on February 24, 1991. Barely 100 hours after the start of the Allied invasion, however, the Iraqi Army was in full retreat and Saddam Hussein was desperate to sue for peace. Meanwhile, much of the Iraqi Air Force had been destroyed on the ground—and the few remaining planes in the air were becoming easy targets for coalition aircraft. On February 27, 1991, President Bush announced the official cease-fire. In their disastrous retreat, the Iraqis had fled Kuwait, leaving a devastated country in their wake. It would take a massive reconstruction effort to get the emirate back on its feet; but for now, the savagery of Iraq's occupation had ended. On March 3, 1991, General H. Norman Schwarzkopf met with several Iraqi generals in Safwan to discuss the terms of surrender.

For the F-15 and F-15E Strike Eagle, the Gulf War had been an opportunity to prove their mettle in the face of the latter-day, Soviet-built aircraft. Indeed, the F-15 had bested the MiGs and Sukhois that she had been designed to counter during the height of the Cold War. In the skies over Iraq, the Eagle had demonstrated its versatility as both a tactical fighter and an attack aircraft. Come what may during the 1990s, the F-15 would remain at the forefront of the post-Cold War military.

Pax Americana

Following the end of Operation Desert Storm, the United States realized that a military presence was still necessary in the Persian Gulf. A Shi'ite rebellion had erupted during the postwar chaos while the Iraqi Kurds (already a targeted minority under the Ba'athist regime) attempted to flee the heavy-handed rule of Saddam Hussein. Thus, to protect the ethnic Kurds in the north, and the Shi'ite Muslims in the south, the US created and enforced "No-Fly Zones" over northern and southern Iraq. Citing UN Resolution 688, the United States mandated that no Iraqi aircraft could enter the No-Fly Zones—else, they would be engaged by hostile fire.

The first aerial patrols over the No-Fly Zone were dubbed "Operation Provide Comfort." During that time (March – July 1991), American F-15 squadrons flew an assortment of combat air patrols and long-range reconnaissance missions. Among the first of these units was the 53d Tactical Fighter Squadron—who had fought valiantly during the air campaign in Desert Storm. On March 20, 1991, nearly one month after the official "cease-fire" ending the Gulf War, Captain John Doneski engaged a wayward Sukhoi Su-22 near Baghdad.

As Doneski's flight leader, Captain Tim Duffy, described it: "Even though the active combat was over, we were still flying CAPs [combat air patrols] over Iraq. The ROE [Rules of Engagement] for this period allowed helicopters to fly, but precluded any fixed-wing flying by the Iraqis." On the afternoon of March 20, Doneski was flying as part of a six-plane formation, tasked to monitor the skies for any unauthorized aircraft. The first few hours of their air patrol were uneventful but, during their in-flight refueling, an egressing F-15 patrol warned Duffy and Doneski of enemy aircraft in the area. As it turned out, these egressing F-15s had detected "multiple Iraqi aircraft on the ramps," surrounded by ground fuelers and other maintenance personnel. This activity suggested one thing: the Iraqi aircraft were preparing to launch.

Acknowledging the transmission, Doneski and his comrades flew around the northeast of Baghdad. "We proceeded west towards a couple of airfields, where there had been a lot of activity," Duffy said, "and then we were going to head over to Al Asad [airbase] for a look. We were cruising at about 20,000 feet."

At 40 miles out, Duffy suddenly picked up a radar contact of an aircraft flying at 4,000

In the aftermath of Operation Desert Storm, the US and its allies continued to patrol Iraqi airspace to enforce the "No-Fly Zone" missions. Here, an American F-15 flies a patrol over the desert immediately following the cease-fire between coalition and Iraqi forces ending Operation Desert Storm. This F-15 is carrying four AIM-9 Sidewinder heatseeking missiles. (US Air Force)

feet with an airspeed of more than 500 knots. Contacting the nearby AWACS, Duffy registered the contact. Although the AWACS had not yet detected any enemy planes in the area, Duffy continued to monitor the activity from his onboard radar.

As the flight group headed north of the Balad Airbase, Duffy directed Doneski to push to the southside of the formation so that the latter could have better radar coverage of that potential threat area. At about 35 miles, Duffy confirmed that the bogey was indeed an Iraqi bandit. "He is heading southeast and we are going due west," Duffy said, "so I check to the left to start to pull some lead."

Moments later, Doneski came on the radio, reporting multiple bogeys coming from the north, down along the Tigris River. Duffy acknowledged the call, but remained focused on the bandit currently populating his F-15's radar. "My bandit is continuing to slow and descend," Duffy said. "This turns out to be his approach and landing." Indeed, the Iraqi plane was landing at the airfield—and once he was on the tarmac, he was legally "safe" from being engaged. "I only get a Tally-Ho on him after he has landed on Runway 32 right at Al Sahra." Duffy, realizing that he had missed his chance to engage the wayward bandit, vectored to the left and climbed to 10,000 feet, continuing to monitor the airfield.

At around this time, Duffy noticed an Su-22 preparing to takeoff from Runway 14R. This lone Sukhoi began taxiing, but suddenly aborted the take-off and jinked his plane into the nearest hangar. Duffy, watching the Sukhoi's hasty retreat, remarked that the Iraqi pilot must have been waved-off by an air traffic controller who had detected the nearby F-15s.

Meanwhile, farther east, Doneski had kept his eye on the incoming bogeys from the north. Focusing on the lead contact—a fixed-wing aircraft at 1,000 feet with an airspeed of 320 knots—Doneski positively identified him as another Su-22.

"Tally-Ho, Fitter!" he called to the nearby AWACS.

The AWACS, however, only acknowledged the call—they gave no transmission indicating whether Doneski was cleared to engage. Taking matters into his own hands, however, Duffy granted Doneski permission to liquidate the target. But before Duffy could even finish saying "cleared to fire," Doneski had already launched his AIM-7.

"At first, all we see is a small flash in the burner can of the Fitter, and it didn't look like it was going to be enough to knock him down. About two seconds later, there is a big fireball out the front as the engine is trashed." The Iraqi ejected, but because his parachute canopy deployed so low to the ground, it was unclear whether the pilot survived the ejection.

Two days later, on March 22, Captain Thomas Dietz downed another Su-22. Like the rest of his comrades in the 53d Fighter Squadron, Dietz was on the lookout for any Iraqi aircraft that were violating the current flight restrictions. "The challenge was to patrol an enormous amount of airspace efficiently, and quickly sort out the helicopters just in case a fighter dared to fly."

On the afternoon of March 22, Dietz and his flight group were approaching the end of their mission when they received the unexpected radar warning of two bogeys travelling at more than 350 knots. "They were too fast to be helicopters," he said, "and the adrenaline immediately ran through my body." Wanting to ensure that his radar

A flight of F-15C Eagles during a routine patrol mission over Iraq in support of Operation Southern Watch. Southern Watch enforced the No-Fly Zone over southern Iraq below the 32d Parallel. These F-15s were part of the 19th and 54th Fighter Squadrons, forward-deployed to Prince Sultan Air Base, Saudi Arabia. (US Air Force)

wasn't malfunctioning, Dietz reset the radar and reacquired the target.

"Sure enough," he said, "350 knots."

Excited at the thought of intercepting an Iraqi fighter, Dietz vectored his F-15 northward and visually acquired the bandit from a distance of five miles. "I could make out a camouflaged paint scheme, a sloped vertical tail, and pointed nose"—the telltale features of an Su-22. As Dietz closed within a mile of his target, he fired an AIM-9 heatseeking missile, brimming as he saw the enemy fighter erupt in a brilliant flash of molten steel. "The heatseeking missile flew right up the target's tail pipe," he said, "and it blew up like in a Hollywood movie."

During the same engagement, Dietz's wingman, Lieutenant Robert Hehemann killed an Iraqi PC-9. This PC-9, however, seemed horribly out of place—for it was a Swiss-built, single-engine turboprop plane comparable to the P-51 Mustang. Dietz and Hehemann could hardly believe their eyes—it wasn't every day that a pilot encountered an enemy formation wherein a Sukhoi jet was being accompanied by a turboprop fighter.

The F-15s continued providing air support throughout subsequent operations over the No-Fly Zones. Operation Provide Comfort II (July 1991—December 1996) continued similar efforts as the first Provide Comfort. The primary objective was to prevent Saddam's ongoing aggression against the Iraqi Kurds. Provide Comfort I and II were successful inasmuch as they facilitated the withdrawal of Iraqi troops from the region in October 1991. Thereafter, the Kurds resumed their autonomy in northern Iraq. At the end of Provide Comfort II, the US launched Operation Northern Watch—a long-term reconnaissance mission over the northern Iraqi No-Fly Zone. Shortly after Provide Comfort I, and almost simultaneously with Provide Comfort II, the US launched Operation Southern Watch—monitoring and controlling Iraqi airspace below the 32d Parallel. Southern Watch was a long-term initiative spanning from July 1992 until the subsequent invasion of Iraq in March 2003.

Despite its initial victories in the skies over post-war Iraq, the F-15 Eagle soon found itself at the center of a terrible fratricide incident. On April 14, 1994, two F-15s—call-signed "Tiger 01" and "Tiger 02"—from the 53d Fighter Squadron departed Incirlik Air Base in Turkey. Their mission was to scan the area for any hostile aircraft violating the No-Fly Zone. The Air Tasking Order (ATO) for that day, which both pilots had read prior to take-off, mentioned that two US Army Blackhawk helicopters would be operating in the area. However, the ATO did not list their take-off times, flight durations, or anticipated routes. At 10:15 AM, the lead F-15 radioed the AWACS, asking for any information regarding other aircraft in the area. But the AWACS had nothing to report.

An F-15E Strike Eagle from the 494th Expeditionary Fighter Squadron flies above the snow-covered mountains during a routine patrol in support of Operation Northern Watch, February 1999. Operation Northern Watch was the coalition enforcement of the Northern No-Fly Zone over Iraq. (US Air Force)

Shortly into their flight, however, Tiger 01 reported radar contact—a slow-moving aircraft, flying at a low altitude approximately 40 miles to his southeast. Unbeknownst to the AWACS and the F-15s, however, this radar contact was one of the two Blackhawks. The AWACS acknowledged the call, but replied that the area was "clean"—meaning they could not identify any hostile aircraft in that location. Initially, the AWACS hadn't even seen the helicopters due to the latter's low altitude and their terrain-masking flight patterns.

Not convinced by the AWACS radio call, Tiger 01 vectored to intercept. At 20 miles out, he again radioed the contact report to the AWACS, who replied with "Hits There"—indicating that the AWACS now saw the radar contacts, too. Using his onboard avionics, Tiger 01 tried to determine whether the slow-moving aircraft was friendly or hostile. When his instrumentation couldn't give him a definitive answer, Tiger 01 moved in for visual identification.

Closing within seven miles, Tiger 01 visually identified the aircraft as a helicopter. Pulling in about 500 feet above the Blackhawk and off to the right, Tiger 01 could see that this helicopter was carrying sponsons, but could not otherwise see any distinguishable markings on the dark green chopper.

Calling back to the AWACS, Tiger 01 misidentified the helicopter as an Iraqi Hind-D. Repositioning himself behind the target, Tiger 01 then noticed the second helicopter. Calling in the second contact, the AWACS—still unaware that these helicopters were actually Blackhawks—simply replied: "Copy Hinds."

Even still, Tiger 01 had his doubts. Contacting his wingman, Tiger 01 asked Tiger 02 to confirm identification. Tiger 02 was his squadron commander, and a decorated pilot with a confirmed kill from Desert Storm. Although Tiger 02 was the squadron commander, the junior-ranking Tiger 01 was the designated "flight lead" for this mission, and thus bore responsibility for all command decisions made during the sortie. This junior-senior pair-up was common as it was designed to give junior pilots more experience in flight leadership.

"Stand by," said Tiger 02.

From 2,000 feet off the right from the trailing helicopter, Tiger 02 called out: "Tally, two."

It was an egregious miscommunication.

In the fighter pilot community, "Tally" meant confirmation of enemy aircraft. Saying "visual," on the other hand, meant that the aircraft were either friendly or unknown. Tiger 02 later testified that he only meant to convey that he had both helicopters in sight.

With that transmission, however, Tiger 01 and Tiger 02 went into their carefully-rehearsed drill of maneuvers to align their shots onto the lead and trail helicopters. "Tiger 01, Fox," said the flight leader as he fired his AIM-120 missile. Closing the four-mile distance, the missile glided straight into the Blackhawk helicopter, crumpling its fuselage into a molten wreck of fire and steel. "Tiger 02 is hot," said the wingman, moments before firing an AIM-9 Sidewinder into the second Blackhawk. The two Blackhawks plummeted into the desert floor, killing all 26 crewmen.

When the tragic outcome came to light, the Air Force initiated a collective court martial. The AWACS crew was blamed for its lack of situational awareness. The lack of detailed information in the ATO cost a high-ranking general his career. Surprisingly,

An F-15E Strike Eagle takes off from Doha International Airport, Qatar, for a morning sortie during Operation Southern Watch. Most of these aerial patrols passed without incident. Occasionally, however, the Iraqi Air Force would send one of its fighters aloft, hoping to provoke coalition aircraft into a chase, and right into an ambush from an air defense missile battery. (US Air Force)

however, the Air Force initially absolved the F-15 pilots of any wrongdoing.

According to aviation photojournalist Steve Davies:

"The F-15 pilots failed in a fundamental fighter pilot responsibility—to be able to correctly visually identify an enemy aircraft from one in their own nation's military—and miscommunicated the ID. Despite the fact that the squadron commander was the wingman…he set the tone for the squadron, he failed to communicate his true (if later testimony is accepted) appreciation for the situation and, if he himself was truly unsure if the targets were friendly or Iraqi, he failed to call of the flight lead until the issue could be resolved with certainty. At 130 knots, the Blackhawks were still 40 miles away from the No-Fly Zone line and were not headed there anyway. There was plenty of time to be sure, but no time was taken.

"Even worse, the USAF handled the tragedy's aftermath appallingly. The two pilots were initially charged with court martial offenses, but rather than allow the merits of each participant's actions to be reviewed by a panel of judges…these were dropped by the commanding general, ostensibly because of insufficient evidence. In fact, the two aviators were given normal, promising assignments for their next tours, until CSAF [Chief of Staff of the Air Force] General Ron Fogleman stepped in and corrected the situation. In the opinion of many, the handling of the case's fallout was almost as much of a black mark against the Air Force as the tragic event itself."

Sadly, the 53d Fighter Squadron, which had distinguished itself so valiantly during Desert Storm, never recovered from the public relations disaster surrounding the Blackhawk shootdown. The unit was subsequently deactivated in March 1999.

An American F-15 from the 363rd Air Expeditionary Wing during an afternoon surveillance mission over the Southern No-Fly Zone. These missions during Operations Northern Watch and Southern Watch were often mundane and repetitive, which prompted several pilots to compare their patrols to the movie *Groundhog Day*. (US Air Force)

Over the ensuing decade, American F-15s regularly patrolled the Iraqi No-Fly Zones. The repetitive nature of these aerial patrols, however, had a corrosive effect on the pilots' morale. In fact, many of them likened their situation to the movie *Groundhog Day*, starring Bill Murray. Given the repetitive nature of these missions, and that the Iraqi Air Force posed no viable threat, these pilots felt that they were simply wasting jet fuel.

Occasionally, however, the Iraqis did push the boundaries of the armistice, launching anti-aircraft fire at the passing F-15s. Most of the Iraqi air defense guns, however, were ineffective beyond 15,000 feet. Thus, the F-15s simply cruised at 20,000 feet or higher, rendering the flak below as nothing more than an entertaining light show.

Radar-guided surface-to-air missiles, however, were another story. Whenever the F-15's SAM alarm went off, evasive maneuvers always followed. On other occasions, the Iraqis would send a MiG within striking distance of an F-15, hoping to provoke the latter into a pursuit, and right into the engagement envelope of a SAM missile battery. These tactics, as the Eagle pilots called them, were "SAMbushes."

One notable example of a SAMbush occurred with Captain Nick Guttman—a two-time veteran of Operation Southern Watch. On his twenty-third mission over Iraq, an AWACS sent him and his wingman to investigate a "track of interest" believed to be a MiG-29. The MiG was flying within the sliver of sovereign Iraqi airspace—and it hadn't yet violated the No-Fly Zone. Still, the coalition wanted to monitor the few MiG-29s that the Iraqis had left. Guttman and his wingman tracked the MiG until it landed, but they were soon alerted to the sound of an incoming Iraqi MIM-23B surface-to-air

Two F-15E Strike Eagles from the 494th Fighter Squadron fly a Combat Air Patrol in support of the NATO No-Fly Zone over Bosnia-Herzegovina, circa 1994. Following the breakup of Yugoslavia, the US and its NATO allies began an air-ground peacekeeping mission to stem the tide of sectarian violence among the various Balkan states. (US Air Force)

missile. Both Guttman and his wingman promptly jettisoned their fuel tanks, and broke away from the engagement area.

But while the F-15C/D struggled to find meaning in the skies over post-war Iraq, the F-15E Strike Eagle was rarely at a loss for potential targets. Although the F-15E scored no aerial victories during Operation Northern Watch and Southern Watch, it did engage several Iraqi air defense sites.

In January 1993, for example, F-15Es from the 4th Fighter Wing (Provisional) led a strike force against Iraqi ground units that had deployed south of the 32d Parallel. During the mission, the F-15Es successfully destroyed an SA-3 missile battery. Occasionally, Iraqi fighters vectored into the No-Fly Zones, but the greater threat came from Iraqi SAMs and other air defense assets.

The pattern of these No-Fly Zone patrols continued uninterrupted until December 16, 1998, when President Bill Clinton authorized Operation Desert Fox—a four-day bombardment of critical Iraqi targets. The stated goal of the operation was to eliminate any sites capable of manufacturing or delivering Weapons of Mass Destruction (WMD). Desert Fox was, at the time, the largest aerial strike against Iraq since the Gulf War. Unfortunately, no F-15s took part in the operation.

Following these hasty bombardments in the Persian Gulf, however, the F-15E Strike Eagles were at their busiest in the spring of 1999. On January 24 of that year, an American F-15E destroyed an Iraqi SA-3 missile site with its AGM-130—a powerful air-to-ground missile. The following day, another Strike Eagle was fired upon by an Iraqi air defense gun. The F-15E quickly returned the favor by dropping a 500-pound GBU-12 bomb. The day after that, two F-15Es fired their AGM-130s, destroying an Iraqi radar site that had been targeting coalition aircraft.

Captain Matt Nicoletta, a young Weapons System Officer (WSO) with the 335th Fighter Squadron, recalled a hair-raising mission during his deployment to Operation Northern Watch in July 1999. "On my first ONW [Northern Watch] sortie, I was shot at," he said, "seeing three white trails to my left." Calling the contact report to his pilot, Nicoletta radioed:

"Missiles in the air, 11 o'clock, check right."

His pilot, a more-experienced aviator, initially dismissed the young back-seater's report.

"Dude, those are roads, not missiles!" the pilot snapped.

However, as Nicoletta kept watching them, he noticed that these "roads" were arcing towards the plane.

"Missiles in the air," he repeated, "Check right, NOW!"

The pilot, now realizing that his WSO had been correct, jerked the plane hard right to avoid the incoming SAMs. "The radios then came alive as everyone started their threat reaction," said Nicoletta, "and I realized that what I should have done was told the whole formation about the missiles." Nicoletta recalled that the typical mission packages

An F-15C Eagle conducts a routine patrol over northern Iraq on December 30, 1998. During these missions over the Iraqi No-Fly Zones, the F-15E Strike Eagle seemed to get most of the action—dodging enemy SAMs and having close encounters with Iraqi MiGs. For the air superiority F-15Cs, however, many of their pilots felt that they were simply "burning holes in the sky." (US Air Force)

included GBU-12s, GBU-10s, AIM-120s, AIM-9s, and AGM-130s—all of which made the Strike Eagle a formidable foe against air and ground targets.

On another mission, Nicoletta recalled an explosion so horrific that it may have rivaled the devastation of Hiroshima. Delivering a GBU-10 to what had been labelled an "ammunition bunker," Nicoletta was shocked when the explosion filled the entire screen of his onboard viewfinder. He had expected a big explosion from the GBU, but nothing *this* big. "There was this billowing mushroom cloud rocketing up through 7,000 feet that sucked up so much dirt that the sky began to darken as it extended up beyond 15,000 feet." Nicoletta's pilot remarked:

"That's one hell of a secondary!"

The pilot's remark was an understatement considering the explosion was so big that the squadron cancelled the rest of the day's missions. Nicoletta never knew precisely what the target had been, but given the enormity of the explosion, he suspected it had to be more than just an "ammunition bunker."

The Balkans

Meanwhile, in the aftermath of Desert Storm, the Socialist Federal Republic of Yugoslavia began to fracture along ethnic and religious lines. A Communist state bordering the Adriatic Sea, Yugoslavia was the dominion of President Josip Broz Tito. Following Tito's death and the collapse of Communism in Eastern Europe, the ethnic and religious groups within Yugoslavia (including Serbs, Croats, et al) began jockeying for independence. These independence movements, however, soon devolved into a civil war—whereupon NATO and the United Nations intervened.

Beginning with Operation Sky Monitor in November 1992, followed by Operation Deny Flight in March 1993, American aircraft gradually increased their role in the skies over Yugoslavia. By the summer of 1993, US aircraft could fly fully-armed close air support missions in support of UN peacekeepers.

Among the first F-15 units to arrive in the Balkans were the 492d and 494th Fighter Squadrons—both of whom flew missions from Aviano Air Base in Italy. During one mission, in the fall of 1993, a group of F-15Es from the 492d flew as part of a 30-aircraft strike force against Serbian ground targets. Armed with GBU-12s, their identified targets were a cluster of SA-6 missile batteries. Sadly, the mission was cancelled mid-flight due to some bureaucratic issue with the Rules of Engagement.

For the first few years of the peacekeeping mission, many F-15 pilots felt like little more than casual observers. Indeed, the heart-pounding sorties of yesteryear were few and far between. In December 1993, for example, a flight of F-15Es destroyed an SA-2 missile site that had fired on two Royal Navy Sea Harriers. Most missions, however, reflected the frustrations of Lieutenant Colonel Michael Arnold, a Strike Eagle pilot who deployed with the 492d Fighter Squadron in 1994. As he recalled: "Most of the missions were very benign and very dull. We enforced the No-Fly Zone, so we would go up and try to engage anyone who was not supposed to be flying, but of course, we never saw anything." Arnold flew several missions armed with CBUs and GBUs, but admitted that he never dropped a single bomb during his deployment. He did, however, get shot at by

F-15 Eagles from the 94th Fighter Squadron return to Langley Air Force Base after a four-month deployment to Turkey, in support of Operation Northern Watch. (US Air Force)

a surface-to-air missile, which he was able to avoid.

Arnold, like many of his comrades were often called upon to do close air support (CAS)—supporting troops with aerial direct fire, often from altitudes of 500 feet or lower. Although the F-15E was, technically, a "strike fighter"—capable of both air superiority and ground attack missions—the dogfighter mentality still pervaded the 492d Squadron's Standard Operating Procedure. "CAS was very new to us back then," he said—"we would hold up the little section in our tactics manual and it would say 'We don't do CAS,' but they soon changed it."

By August 1995, NATO planes had become more aggressive in their enforcement of Operation Deny Flight. After NATO initiated its bombing campaign on Sarajevo, American F-15Es dropped their GBU-10s and GBU-12s onto select targets on September 5. Four days later, another F-15E destroyed a Bosnian Serb target with its GBU-15 electro-optically guided bomb. This marked the first time that the GBU-15 had been used in combat.

In March 1999, NATO began yet another military operation in the former Yugoslavia, this time in Kosovo. NATO—already having a foothold in the region due to its peacekeeping missions in Bosnia—was determined to drive the Yugoslavs from Kosovo on the grounds of humanitarian intervention. To affect these goals, the F-15 Eagle and Strike Eagle once again returned to the fray. The new mission was dubbed: "Operation Allied Force."

"Air operations in Allied Force," said Lieutenant Colonel Will Reece, "had two main aims. The first was interdiction in order to keep the Serbian Army out of Kosovo. The second was CAS." As the Weapons Officer for the 492d Fighter Squadron, Reece said

An F-15E Strike Eagle pilot from the 494th Fighter Squadron, undergoes a pre-flight check on his aircraft prior to NATO air strikes on Serbian targets surrounding Sarajevo, Bosnia-Herzegovina, August 1995. (US Air Force)

that although CAS is a common practice in today's fighter squadrons, "it was very new to us in 1999." For missions over the Balkans, the typical flight stores included GBU-10, GBU-12, and/or GBU-24 bombs, along with a few air-to-air missiles should any Serbian MiGs wish to engage.

During Allied Force, the F-15E was the only NATO aircraft to fly in all types of weather, day and night. It was also during this time that the F-15Es first used night-vision devices (NVDs) in combat. Another significant milestone for the Strike Eagle was its dual role during the conflict. As a true "strike fighter," the F-15E fulfilled the roles of close air support *and* combat air patrols. On the occasion that an F-15E flew without NVDs, the Strike Eagle would work in concert with the F-16 Fighting Falcon, using a technique known as "buddy lasing." Under this method, the F-15E would drop its GBUs, and a nearby F-16 would guide the bomb to target by using its onboard laser.

While patrolling the skies over Bosnia, Serbia, and other hots spots in the former Yugoslavia, the greatest threat came from the enemy's air defense forces. Indeed, the Balkan air forces and their air defense troops had derived their tactics from the latter-day Soviets. The discriminating factor, however, was the Yugoslavs' tenacity and their willingness to fight while being outnumbered.

The main problem facing the Strike Eagles and their NATO counterparts was the high concentration of mobile SA-6 launchers. Having learned lessons from the Iraqis following Desert Storm, "Milosevic's forces were cunning in their use of deception and self-control"—hiding their best missile launchers and waiting to fire until conditions were ideal.

As Lieutenant Colonel Reece recalled: "Daily pre-flight briefs focused heavily on mobile SAM locations. The intelligence collectors were smart, but the Serbs were smart too, and they had learned a lot from the Iraqis." In fact, the Serbs frequently moved their SAM launchers. "We sometimes got surprised," he said, "but the reality is that with the systems we have in the F–15E, I can beat the SA-6 if I can see it. It's the one I can't see that gets me."

While the F–15E Strike Eagles pounded Serbian targets from the air, the F–15C resumed its role as the king of aerial combat. During Allied Force, the Federal Republic of Yugoslavia Air Force sent its ailing fleet of MiG-29s to intercept NATO aircraft operating within Yugoslav airspace. By 1999, however, there was little that this fleet could actually accomplish.

Following the breakup of the original Yugoslavia, the national air force had shrunk to one-third of its former size. Subsequent to the Dayton Peace Accords in 1995, the Yugoslav Air Force reduced its numbers even further. Thus, by the time Allied Force began, they had barely sixty MiG-21s and sixteen MiG-29s. Even before the war, the Yugoslav government had struggled to keep its fleet of MiG-29s operational. Therefore, it seemed inevitable that these ailing MiGs would meet their demise against the incoming F–15s.

On March 24, 1999, Cesar Rodriguez (now a Lieutenant Colonel)—the man who had downed two Iraqi MiGs while flying with the 58th Fighter Squadron in Desert Storm—scored his *third* kill while over the city of Pristina. Now as a member of the

A maintenance handler gathers safety pins and wheel chocks as an F–15C Eagle from the 53rd Fighter Squadron prepares to take flight on a mission to enforce the No-Fly Zone over Bosnia-Herzegovina, 1995. (US Air Force)

Through the green aura of the night vision device, this photograph captures the F-15 Eagle during its aerial refueling while on another mission over the former Yugoslavia. (US Air Force)

493d Fighter Squadron, he flew from RAF Lakenheath to Aviano Air Base with his wingmen—many of whom were young and untested. In light of their youth, however, these untested wingmen would perform remarkably in their first combat sorties.

"There were two missions on this first night," said Rodriguez, "both spearheaded by F-15s of the 493d Fighter Squadron." The targets for this mission were primarily in Montenegro—radar and air defense sites positioned to deny access to Pristina. "The strike was designed to break a hole in this SAM belt, and to open access for the CAS assets that needed to get into Kosovo from the west."

That night, Rodriguez flew as part of a four-plane formation. His wingman was the young Lieutenant William Denim (callsign: "Wild Bill"). Coincidentally, Denim was one of the youngest pilots in the squadron. He had just completed his "check rides" and had logged less than 100 hours of flight time in the F-15. "In fact," Rodriguez said, "he would finish the war with more combat time than peacetime flying in the F-15, and like all our young aviators, he did just phenomenal work."

Heading north towards Montenegro, Rodriguez and his wingman found an initial radar contact 25 miles from a templated airfield. At first, it appeared to be an enemy air patrol, but its orbiting flight pattern and slow airspeed suggested that it wasn't a fighter patrol. While the flight leader focused on this enemy flight group, Rodriguez and Denim maintained their focus on Pristina. "Our main task was to ensure that nothing took off from Pristina heading towards Montenegro that might intercept our strike."

Suddenly, from a distance of 70 miles, Rodriguez got radar contact of a fast mover climbing to 10,000 feet. With his onboard instrumentation, Rodriguez confirmed that

An F-15E Strike Eagle takes off from Aviano Air Base, Italy, for a strike mission in support of Operation Allied Force on March 28, 1999. (US Air Force)

this lurking bandit was a MiG-29. "I directed my element to start a climb, jettison tanks, and push it up. This would give our [missiles] greater range and since we were on the front edge of the strike package, I wanted to shoot as soon as possible…start the shooting match on our terms, not the MiG's."

Closing within 20 miles, Rodriguez fired an AIM-120 missile. Rodriguez hadn't realized it, but he had accelerated to Mach 1.3. Thus, as the missile glided off his wing, it appeared as though the AIM-120 was flying alongside him. "The missile took a couple of seconds to build up momentum and accelerate out in front of me, and during that time, I thought I might have had a bad missile." As the missile plowed forward into the night, Rodriguez could see the faint glow of the MiG-29's engine—"about the size of a dime," he recalled.

As he looked through his sights, he lost visual contact of the MiG, as it was dark outside. "But I was counting down the seconds left for the missile to impact." As the counter reached zero, a huge fireball erupted. "Because the western mountains were still covered in snow," he continued, "the fireball literally lit up the sky as it reflected off the snow-covered mountains. The only thing I had ever seen like this was when they turn on all the lights at an NFL stadium, except this was like five times that bright; it really lit up the whole sky. In fact, an F-15E WSO about 85 miles to the southwest of my fireball, heard my "Splash" call and simultaneously saw the bright glow. He became suspicious of what might have detonated up there, since the glow was so bright! As it turned out, it was just that MiG-29 exploding."

Reflecting on his mission in the Balkans, Rodriguez said: "Operation Allied Force represented a turning point in the understanding of warfare by the average fighter pilot. As one of a few Desert Storm veterans in our squadron, I kind of felt it was my responsibility to help guys understand their role in actual combat, and the impact of combat on our squadron…and our families back home. I also made a point to help the young guys understand the political ramifications of being armed with an air-to-air machine, and that you are sending a political statement any time you hit that pickle button.

"Allied Force represented a political tightrope, where US forces and NATO forces were coming together for a political objective. We realized at that point that NATO had fallen behind in its training and technological investment. As a result, some of the tactics that were employed had to be 'watered down' significantly so that other partners could play completely in the entire operation. We also had a unique scenario where, as the US leadership from SHAPE [Supreme Headquarters, Allied Powers Europe] was directing airpower, they were not always airmen, and hence sometimes that direction was poor. It was common to go after targets that had already been struck, or going after targets that had no impact on forcing Yugoslavia to surrender."

Rodriguez concluded: "I say it was a turning point because, unlike Desert Storm, where we had no idea what was going on, we were just the execution element, we were actively involved in planning the air campaign over Yugoslavia. Unfortunately, when these recommendations got to SHAPE, they were often changed, and airmen were put into harm's way striking targets that had no significance. But that's a whole other aspect

An F-15E Strike Eagle takes off from Aviano Air Base, Italy, for a strike mission in support of Operation Allied Force on March 28, 1999. (US Air Force)

of this battle space. The actions of the 493d were significant in developing tactics for both day and night employment that are still used by the F-15 community."

That same night, one of Rodriguez's comrades, Captain Michael Shower (callsign: "Dozer") downed his own MiG-29. Dozer had gone aloft with an assortment of other NATO aircraft—all of which were operating within a tight airspace. "The B-2s [stealth bombers] were moving south to north throughout the country, so they were really under everyone's protection during the mission. The F-117s [stealth fighters] were doing their 'spider routes' going all over to their various targets in northern Serbia." According to Shower, his mission was to fly as part of a two-plane formation and set up a Combat Air Patrol north of Belgrade. "This would keep us out of the SAM rings, but give us good coverage of their known MiG bases."

Settling into his patrol, Shower heard the radio erupt with "Splash one MiG in the south!"—confirming Rodriguez's kill of the MiG-29.

Shower was excited.

"We had questioned whether they [the MiGs] would fly or not," he said, "and now we knew the MiGs were up." He had been over Serbian airspace for all of seven minutes, and there was now enemy contact. His excitement intensified the moment he saw a radar contact of his own—35 miles from his position, a fast-moving aircraft was climbing up to 10,000 feet. "By 17 miles, I have an ID that this is a bad guy and I call it out." Arming his missiles, Shower bellowed: "Hostile! Hostile! Fox 3!"—firing an AIM-120 from a distance of fourteen miles.

As soon as the AIM-120 left the missile rack, Shower thumbed the selector switch to AIM-7 and fired a Sparrow missile. "I'm looking down into the lights of Belgrade, so I can't see anything, but I was able to follow the missile motor for a little while." Sadly, both missiles failed to lock on to the fleeting MiG.

Closing withing five and a half miles, Shower fired another AIM-120 and watched in amazement as the missile impacted the MiG. "I don't see an ejection, but there was a lot of stuff coming off the aircraft, and I watched it impact on the ground. We later found out that the pilot actually survived, which I was glad about…he had a wife and kids, too." In fact, the MiG pilot was later identified as Major Nebojsa Nikolic, who later wrote an article describing his experiences being shot down.

Two days later, Captain Jeff Hwang (also assigned to the 493d Fighter Squadron) downed two MiG-29s over Bosnia. At 4:02 PM, Hwang and his wingman were eastbound, approaching the Bosnia-Serbia border, when they got a radar contact 37 miles out, closing at 600 knots. "Of course, the AWACS had no clue, and did not have any inkling someone was flying on the other side of the border," said Hwang.

Not thinking much about the contact, and not being in a good position to cross the border, Hwang and his wingman vectored southward and continued to monitor the radar contact. "I figured the contact would probably continue south or turn east and remain well south of the border." Still, Hwang alerted the AWACS of the contact and he passed a similar report to his flight leader, who was conducting another aerial patrol over Sarajevo.

"This entire time," said Hwang, "AWACS still had no radar contact, even after I called

Colonel Jeff Hwang, as seen after his last flight aboard the F-15C Eagle in 2014. As a young Captain, Hwang destroyed two Serbian MiG-29s during Operation Allied Force in 1999. These kills are denoted by the green stars painted on his fuselage. At the time of this picture, Hwang was flying with the Oregon Air National Guard. (US Air Force)

it out on the radio. Man, running away with the contact at our six o'clock with AWACS not having any clue was NOT comfortable!"

A few moments later, Hwang once again got radar contact of the incoming bogey, who was now headed straight for them. "AWACS finally woke up and saw the same thing." From the bogey's relative position, Hwang could tell it was a Yugoslav fighter. However, given the Rules of Engagement for today's mission, he needed clearance from the AWACS before firing. Hwang radioed the AWACS with the designated "code word"—indicating a request to engage a hostile target.

The AWACS, however, remained silent.

At this point, Hwang was certain that the AWACS "had no freakin' clue what the code word meant!" Once the target closed within 30 nautical miles, Hwang decided he wasn't going to wait for the AWACS to grant permission. Vectoring northeast, Hwang and his wingman gained visual contact on the bandits almost as soon as the AWACS confirmed that the incoming planes were MiGs.

Closing within 16 nautical miles, Hwang fired his first missile. "The missile came off with a loud roar/whoosh," he said, "I not only heard it in the cockpit above the wind noise, radio comms, ear plugs, and helmet, I actually FELT the rocket motor roar!" Hwang then fired a second missile.

"Fox 6! Lead Trail!" he cried as the missile glided off its rail.

Diving down from 30,000 feet, Hwang then acquired the trailing jet in his sights. He was about to line up an AIM-9 missile shot when, suddenly, he saw the first plane explode—a victim of one of Hwang's first two missiles. "The best visual description I can think of is if you've held a torch from one of those Hawaiian luau parties and swung it through the air. The flame, with an extended tail trailing the torch, is exactly what I saw!" Seconds later, Hwang saw the trailing jet explode.

Satisfied that both jets had been destroyed, Hwang un-selected the AIM-9, which he had intended to be his third missile shot of the afternoon. It was later confirmed that although Hwang's wingman fired first, it was both of Hwang's missiles that destroyed the respective bandits. Both Serbian pilots ejected, but only one survived the ejection.

The mission in Kosovo ended on June 10, 1999—but the ongoing tensions with Iraq had not yet subsided. Even before the air campaign in Kosovo had begun, the Iraqi Air Force continued to challenge the No-Fly Zones. Most of these confrontations ended without incident. Tensions, however, remained high over the next few years, and these aerial cat-and-mouse games continued until the 2003 invasion of Iraq.

This Kind of War

On September 20, 2001, President George W. Bush addressed the American people from the US Capitol and announced, "Tonight, we are country awakened to danger and called to defend freedom. Our grief has turned to anger and anger to resolution." His remarks were in reference to the terrorist attacks on New York City and Washington DC on September 11. It was a dastardly, premeditated act of terror—the likes of which the United States had never seen. This attack on US soil,

An F-15E Strike Eagle sits at Bagram Air Field, Afghanistan. This Strike Eagle, Number 89-0487, is the same aircraft flown by Captains Richard Bennett and Dan Bakke during Operation Desert Storm. This aircraft was credited with the first and only air-to-air kill for the Strike Eagle, downing an Iraqi helicopter in February 1991. At the time of this photograph, this Strike Eagle had logged more than 10,000 hours of flight time. (US Air Force)

perpetrated by the al-Qaeda terrorist group, rallied the country to retaliate. In the weeks following September 11, the recurring themes of "justice" and "freedom" resounded through America's political discourse. These concepts stood in direct contrast to the radical, Islamic fundamentalism of al-Qaeda and the countries that harbored its ranks.

In the case of September 11, al-Qaeda had been aided and abetted by the Taliban regime—a brutal Islamic theocracy that had taken over Afghanistan in the wake of the Soviets' departure. President Bush continued highlighting the contrast between the freedoms of the West and the brutality of the Taliban as he declared the start of a "Global War on Terror."

The United States was now on the offensive.

Likewise, President Bush declared that, going forward, "any nation that continues to harbor or support terrorism will be regarded by the United States as a hostile regime." Approximately two weeks later, the first American airstrikes began in Afghanistan—the official start of Operation Enduring Freedom.

Leading up to these airstrikes, however, the US demanded the immediate closing of training camps in Afghanistan and the deliverance of al-Qaeda leader Osama Bin Laden to US authorities. "These demands are not open to negotiation or discussion," said President Bush. "The Taliban must act and act immediately. They will hand over the terrorists, or they will share in their fate."

All told, the US knew that the Taliban would never comply with these demands. Thus, as early as September 12, the Department of Defense began discussing its options for war. Given Afghanistan's location, responsibility for theater-level operations would fall to the United States Central Command (CENTCOM). CENTCOM determined that a combination of efforts were needed to make any headway in Afghanistan—air power, Special Forces, and building alliances with indigenous militant groups opposed to the Taliban. Al-Qaeda and the Taliban were unconventional enemies; thus the US needed an unconventional approach. Unlike during Desert Storm, American forces were not fighting a conventional near-peer threat. This time, the enemy was an unconventional group hiding both in the wilderness and amongst the population. As Secretary of Defense Donald Rumsfeld said: "There's no question that there are any number of people in Afghanistan—tribes in the south and the Northern Alliance in the north—that oppose the Taliban, and clearly we need to recognize the value they bring to this anti-terrorist, anti-Taliban effort, and where possible find ways to assist them."

Much of this assistance would come from the skies, where the F-15E Strike Eagle would play an indispensable role. While the air superiority F-15 Eagles flew aerial patrols protecting American cities and potential stateside targets, the F-15E Strike Eagles headed east to meet the Taliban. On October 12, 2001, twelve F-15Es from the 391st Fighter Squadron departed Mountain Home Air Force Base, Idaho en route to Ahmed Al Jaber Air Base, Kuwait. Once there, they fell under command of the 332d Air Expeditionary Group.

Combat sorties began in mid-October. From the outset, Squadron leaders and flight crews knew that Afghanistan would offer little, if any, fixed targets of appreciable value. Therefore, as Lieutenant Colonel Andrew Dritschgi, commander of the 391st, noted: "We knew we'd end up working with FAC [forward air controllers] if we were ever tasked to strike targets in Afghanistan." Later that month, the 391st Fighter Squadron

Maintenance personnel watch as an F–15E from the 391st Fighter Squadron prepares to launch from Al Udeid Air Base, Qatar. The Strike Eagle is carrying a rack of GBU–12 500-pound bombs and is preparing first bombing mission into Afghanistan, October 2001. (US Air Force)

An American F-15E Strike Eagle conducting a "show of force" mission over Afghanistan. The F-15Es frequently performed fly-overs of this nature to deter enemy activity and protect coalition forces on the ground. (US Air Force)

led the first Strike Eagle attacks, meeting only piecemeal resistance over their assigned targets. This began a continuous cycle of F-15E sorties that ran nearly 24 hours a day for the next three months. As one Weapons Systems Officer (WSO) recalled: "For the first fortnight or so, military buildings, Taliban supply depots, caves, and Al-Qaeda training camps were the focus of our attack."

By the end of October, the Strike Eagles had dropped several thousand pounds of AGM-130 and EGBU-15—the latter of which was a GPS-guided version of the earlier GBU-15. Other air-to-ground assets included the GBU-24 and GBU-28. The former was a 2,000-pound laser-guided bomb, while the latter was designated a "bunker buster"—used for destroying cave complexes and other reinforced positions held by the Taliban.

> "Within a matter of weeks, mission planners were discovering that they had almost exhausted their list of meaningful fixed targets in Afghanistan—repair of the country's military infrastructure had never been a priority for the Taliban. At this point, Strike Eagles began flying more Time Sensitive Tasking (TST) missions, TST targets being those that could move or hide if they were not attacked within a certain window of opportunity—ie people, vehicles, etc."

When troops in contact needed close air support (CAS), the Strike Eagles were quick to respond. Most of these CAS missions, however, happened at night, when the Taliban felt safe to move around. Moreover, many of these CAS calls came from Special Forces FACs who were fighting alongside the Northern Alliance, attempting to flush the Taliban out from their mountainous citadels.

While being talked on to these targets by the local FACs, the Strike Eagles would fly exceptionally low to identify the target area and distinguish friendly troops from hostiles. These CAS missions also lent themselves to some enterprising tactics. For example, when responding to a Special Forces call to destroy a convoy of Taliban trucks crossing a bridge, the FAC added a request that the bridge itself not be destroyed, lest the Northern Alliance need to use it later. Normally, such a request would have elicited a hearty guffaw from the pilot, followed by an assertion that he couldn't destroy the trucks without also destroying the bridge—the ever-present notion of "collateral damage."

But today, the obliging F-15E pilot rolled his jet skyward, and skillfully dove down to destroy the convoy with a burst from his 20mm autocannon.

The bridge remained intact.

And the pilot's maneuver had validated the utility of the Strike Eagle's gun as an offensive weapon for supporting ground troops.

In January 2002, the 391st Fighter Squadron returned to the United States—"having achieved a sortie generation rate of 85%, flying two to eight sorties every day." Taking their place on the Afghan battlefront was the 335th Fighter Squadron, deploying from Seymour Johnson Air Force Base, North Carolina.

Still on the hunt for al-Qaeda leaders and Osama bin Laden, US intelligence looked for regions that would provide attack and defensive positions. In February 2002, analysts began focusing on the lower Shah-i-Kot Valley. Standing at an average elevation of 9,000 feet, this rugged valley had been the site of an intense battle between Soviet Airborne

An F-15E Strike Eagle from the 335th Fighter Squadron drops a 2,000-pound Joint Direct-Attack Munition (JDAM) bomb on a cave in eastern Afghanistan, 2009. While the air-superiority F-15Cs largely remained stateside, defending American skies, the F-15E Strike Eagle units regularly deployed to Afghanistan, engaging the Taliban and Al Qaeda with a variety of precision-guided munitions. (US Air Force)

Troops and the *Mujahedeen* in January 1988. Fortified with bunkers and offering excellent redoubts, US analysts believed that enemy forces from Tora Bora had escaped to the Lower Shah-i-Kot Valley and were planning to regroup against the US-led coalition. Thus, American forces began devising a plan to flush the enemy out of the Shah-i-Kot. It was to be called Operation Anaconda.

Anaconda featured a mix of conventional ground forces with close air support. On the ground were 2,000 soldiers from the US Army's 10th Mountain Division and 101st Airborne Division. Additionally, allied Afghan forces supplemented the operation with their own indigenous fighters. This US-Afghan force intended the destruction of all enemy units within seventy-two hours. Operation Anaconda commenced on March 1, 2002, beginning with US Special Forces teams sweeping the outskirts of the valley.

It was during the throes of Operation Anaconda that the 335th Fighter Squadron would prove its mettle.

On March 4, 2002, a section of F-15Es—call-signed "Twister 51" and "Twister 52"—joined the melee of what became known as the Battle of Roberts' Ridge. This battle, as it were, became one of the focal points of Operation Anaconda. The "Twister" Strike Eagles had been aloft for nearly four hours conducting an on-call CAS mission. Their mission stores included nine GBU-12s, more than 500 rounds of PBU-28 bullets, and a handful of air-to-air missiles just in case they met any hostile aircraft.

At 1:25 AM, Twister 51 and 52 got an urgent call from the AWACS to contact a local FAC, call-signed "Texas 14." The FAC talked them onto an enemy mortar position—which the F-15Es promptly silenced with a GBU-12. Then, an unknown caller who identified himself as "Mako 30" came on the radio, requesting support against an enemy mortar position 600 yards to his west.

From the content and delivery of the radio transmission, Twister 51 and 52 could tell that Mako 30 was not an Air Force-trained FAC. He wasn't using the standard 9-line Close Air Support brief.

It was later confirmed that Mako 30 was actually a Navy SEAL.

He had been trying to recover a fellow SEAL, Neil Roberts, whom had fallen from the back of a Chinook helicopter. In the scramble to help the beleaguered SEAL team, another Chinook (carrying a rescue team) was downed by a Taliban RPG. Thus Twister 51 and 52 were now rendering CAS to the SEALs *and* the crew of the downed helicopter.

To stave off the enemy, the Strike Eagles made multiple strafing runs. Another FAC—using the callsign "Slick 01," brought in the Strike Eagles using the downed helicopter as a common reference point. As the F-15Es rained fire on the Taliban positions, Captain Chris Russell, the WSO aboard Twister 52, heard the FAC cry:

"Good guns! I can smell the trees!"

Essentially, the F-15E's gunfire had split the nearby pine trees and the FAC could smell the sap.

Throughout the mission that day, Twister 51 and 52 stayed aloft for more than 12 hours. As Lieutenant Colonel James Fairchild, the WSO aboard Twister 51 recalled: "Those kids were on the ground for 15 hours before they were finally pulled out. People have made a lot out of what we did that day, but in my opinion, the real heroes of the day, were the guys on the ground fighting to stay alive."

An F-15E Strike Eagle from the 391st Expeditionary Fighter Squadron launches heat decoys during a close-air-support mission over Afghanistan, December 2008. (US Air Force)

Also during Operation Anaconda, the 335th debuted the new BLU-118B thermobaric bomb. "Lauded by the international press as a grisly weapon that burned the oxygen from the lungs of its victims, this thermobaric bomb was seen as the solution to the coalition's main problem at the time—flushing out Taliban fighters hidden deep inside a cave complex."

Although Operation Anaconda was a tactical victory for American forces, it highlighted the need for tight inter-service communication and better intelligence. An operation intended to last 72 hours ended up running a total of eighteen days. The US saw eight servicemen killed, 72 wounded, and lost two Chinook helicopters. In the end, US forces pushed the Taliban and al-Qaida from the valley, but Osama bin Laden remained at large and no major captures or kills had been confirmed.

The intrepid F-15E Strike Eagle squadrons continued flying CAS missions well into the next decade. However, their participation in Operation Enduring Freedom would not be limited only to Afghanistan. Indeed, operations in an around the Horn of Africa necessitated the use of F-15E strikes from Djibouti-Ambouli International Airport. From there, Strike Eagles have supported ongoing operations against terrorists in both the Arabian Peninsula and Africa proper.

In June 2011, President Obama addressed the American people regarding "The Way Forward" strategy for Afghanistan. "We start the drawdown of US troops from a position of strength," he said. "We have exceeded our expectations on our core goal of defeating al-Qaeda, and the killing of its top 30 leaders, including Osama bin Laden. We have broken the Taliban's momentum, and trained over 100,000 Afghan National Security

F-15E Strike Eagle on patrol in Afghanistan on October 7, 2008. With its vast capabilities, the F-15E can fight at low altitudes, day or night, and any kind of weather. (US Air Force)

Forces." Subsequent to this announcement, the US Department of Defense initiated the withdrawal of 10,000 troops from Afghanistan.

In December 2014, after thirteen years of combat missions, President Obama declared the end of Operation Enduring Freedom. The proclamation, however, was largely symbolic, as the remaining US troops were soon categorized under a new mission known as "Operation Freedom's Sentinel." Essentially, Operation Freedom's Sentinel picked up where Enduring Freedom left off—at this writing, US troops are still engaged in combat against remnants of the Taliban. Airstrikes by US and coalition forces continue to this day.

Operation Iraqi Freedom/New Dawn

Continuing the Global War on Terror, the United States next turned its attention towards Iraq. Under the newly-articulated Bush Doctrine, the United States would pursue a policy of pre-emptive action against any country that harbored terrorists or likely posed a threat to American security. "If we wait for threats to fully materialize," the President said, "we will have waited too long." To this end, the US prosecuted its case against Saddam Hussein's Iraq.

Following the end of the Gulf War in 1991, US-Iraqi relations remained at an all-time low. The economic sanctions and No-Fly Zones were only the most visible reminders of this lingering animosity. Indeed, since his defeat at the hands of the US military, Saddam had increased his support for terrorism, and orchestrated a number of terrorist plots himself. One audacious plot involved an assassination attempt on former President

George HW Bush. To make matters worse, Saddam had defied multiple UN sanctions and expelled UN weapons inspectors from Iraq. Thus, it came as little surprise when the international community renewed its interest in assessing Iraq's ability to create Weapons of Mass Destruction (WMD). These weapons included Mustard Gas, VX, Sarin, and the normal variety of nuclear munitions.

To initiate action against Iraq, however, the United States had to build the case for an invasion. Working with the United Nations, a series of weapons factory inspections took place in Iraq throughout 2002. In turn, the UN passed resolutions demanding Iraq's disarmament. The weapons inspection, however, yielded inconclusive results. The inspectors recorded several abnormalities and oddly-missing components that were vital to the creation of WMDs. Meanwhile, Deputy Secretary of Defense Paul Wolfowitz conceded that there were other concerns:

> "The truth is that, for reasons that have a lot to do with the US government bureaucracy, we settled on the one issue that everyone could agree on, which was weapons of mass destruction as the core reason, but, there have always been three fundamental concerns. One is weapons of mass destruction, the second is support for terrorism, the third is the criminal treatment of the Iraqi people. Actually, I guess you could say there's a fourth overriding one which is the connection between the first two."

With his purpose clear, President Bush looked to Congress for approval. Before a joint session of Congress, Bush argued that "the gathering threat of Iraq must be confronted fully and finally." Thus, on October 3, 2002, the House and Senate authorize the use of

A Strike Eagle from the 391st Fighter Squadron during its in-flight refueling over the snowy mountains of Afghanistan. (US Air Force)

military force against Iraq.

Having received Congressional approval, Bush then sent Secretary of State Colin Powell to the United Nations, accelerating America's effort to gain the blessing of the international community. On February 5, 2003, in front of the UN General Assembly, Powell artfully presented his case. He argued that, "the moment we find ourselves in now is a critical moment where we are being tested and where the Security Council of the United Nations and the international community is being tested." He provided what seemed like evidence that Iraq was still manufacturing WMDs. Powell further argued that Saddam's defiance of past resolutions would undermine the UN's credibility. Accordingly, he warned that the United Nations would become "irrelevant if it passes resolution after resolution that is simply totally ignored by a country in a situation where that country continues to develop weapons of mass destruction."

Although sincere and passionate in his presentation, Colin Powell failed to win support from the United Nations. Although there was much dissent within the General Assembly, the US had still won a number of allies to its cause. There would be no UN resolution, but allies such as the United Kingdom and Australia pledged their support. Seemingly undeterred by the UN's lack of enthusiasm, President Bush stated that if Saddam Hussein did not disarm, the United States would "lead a coalition of the willing to disarm him and at that point in time, all our nations...will be able to choose whether or not they want to participate." This "coalition of the willing" eventually grew to include more than 40 allies. Meanwhile, CIA operatives and Special Forces troops had been in Iraq for months, preparing and performing reconnaissance for what would become Operation Iraqi Freedom (OIF).

Against the eerie glow of an electrical storm, this F-15E stands silhouetted at Bagram Air Base in Afghanistan. (US Air Force)

An F-15E Strike Eagle from the 494th Fighter Squadron takes flight from RAF Lakenheath on a deployment to the Middle East in support of Operation Iraqi Freedom—July 14, 2003. (US Air Force)

In 2002, as President Bush continued building the case for war, the US Air Force installed the new Flight Data Link (FDL) system into its F-15C/D and F-15E models. FDL collated communication, navigation, and real-time information to all aircraft in-theater. FDL augmented situational awareness for NATO pilots by giving them real-time data to aid them in the execution of their mission plans.

In December of that year, the 4th Fighter Wing, stationed at Seymour Johnson Air Force Base, North Carolina—and operators of the world's largest fleet of F-15E Strike Eagles—received the alert to deploy to the Persian Gulf in January 2003. They would be headed for Al Udeid Air Base in Qatar.

The 336th Fighter Squadron ("Rocketeers") were the first of the 4th Fighter Wing's elements to arrive in the region, followed soon thereafter by their "sister unit," the 335th Fighter Squadron ("Chiefs"). From these two squadrons, a total of 48 aircraft arrived as the initial contingent of F-15Es to Qatar in January 2003.

At this time, the US Navy and Air Force were still flying sorties under Operation Southern Watch. Thus, for the 335th and 336th Fighter Squadrons, their initial flight plans were sculpted from those found in the Southern Watch ATOs. However, these Southern Watch flyovers soon began focusing on NTISR—non-traditional intelligence, surveillance, and reconnaissance. These NTISR missions included information-gathering, locating enemy positions and exposing their strengths, and targeting air defense systems in Iraq.

Because the Strike Eagles were operating within Qatari airspace, the F-15E pilots occasionally had to yield to their host-nation flight leads. Indeed, sometimes the Qatari pilots would give the mission directives for any given day. For the American pilots, however, listening to their Qatari counterparts was a humorous affair. For example, one of the Qatari Mirage pilots led a briefing that began like this:

"You listen to me talk, or you no fly in Qatar."

An F–15E Strike Eagle departs after completing its in-flight refuel during another mission over the Persian Gulf. (US Air Force)

"I am good pilot, trust me."

"Mirage Dash–5 is excellent airplane and we can zoom up to 40,000 feet."

It was clear to the F–15E crewmen that this Qatari pilot had little command of the English language—his speech was stilted, wooden, and sounded almost nonsensical. One American pilot remarked: "At the time we saw the Strike Eagle guys snicker, but you could actually *hear* the F–16 guys roll their eyes."

Diplomatic *faux pas* notwithstanding, the F–15E Strike Eagles and F–16 Fighting Falcons soon settled into a regular rhythm of aerial patrolling. For their NTISR missions, the Strike Eagles used their new FDL pods to look for any potential Iraqi targets. These sorties were flown under the banner of Strike Familiarization (SFAM) with live weapons, ready to be launched should the Combined Air Operations Center (CAOC) divert them onto a strike mission instead.

As Captain Joe Siberski, who served as a WSO instructor in the 336th, recalled:

"NITSR as I knew it started when I was the CAOC. One day this intel captain comes up to me with an idea that he had already pitched to some 'higher-ups.' Apparently they bought it, and now he was trying to make it work. His idea—I don't know if it was an original thought or not—was that we would recce [reconnoiter] places on our 'strike fams' with the pods. He said he could not get conventional assets over a fraction of the sites he wanted with the timeline he needed, but we 'Strikes' (F–15Es) flew over them all the time. So, he bounced ideas off me. I gave him my opinion and voila, it's in the 'frag' [fragmentary order] the next day. He was a real cool dude, and sharp as all hell. I don't think he ever slept. I don't know how he did it. Even though he was so overworked, he always managed to find time to help me out whenever I needed intel assistance."

Once their routines had been established, the 335th and 336th Fighter Squadrons recalled that Qatar was a relaxing place to work. Some remarked that the Qatari aviation community was so laid-back that they allowed flights into areas that were clearly marked prohibited. The only drawback, it seemed was that Qatar had no active bomb range—thus the Strike Eagles had no feasible area to practice strafing runs or other ground-attack maneuvers.

However, within days of commencing their normal flight operations, the 336th Fighter Squadron was formally tasked to begin flying Strike Coordination Attack and Reconnaissance (SCAR) missions. Under the SCAR concept, the F-15Es would monitor and assess targets before handing them off to other strike formations. SCAR was similar to the US Navy's "hunter-killer team" concept practiced by F-14s and F/A-18s working in tandem. These F-14 Tomcats would find ("hunt") the targets; then pass them off to the F/A-18 Hornets, who would "kill" the designated target.

The military invasion of Iraq began on March 20, 2003 and had a wide-sweeping agenda with eight objectives. According to US Army General Tommy Franks, these objectives were as follows:

"First, ending the regime of Saddam Hussein. Second, to identify, isolate, and eliminate Iraq's weapons of mass destruction. Third, to search for, to capture, and to drive out terrorists from that country. Fourth, to collect such intelligence as we can relate to terrorist networks. Fifth, to collect such intelligence as we can relate to the global network of illicit weapons of mass destruction. Sixth, to end sanctions and to immediately deliver humanitarian support. Seventh, to secure Iraq's oil fields and resources, which belong to the Iraqi people. And last, to help the Iraqi people create conditions for a transition to a representative self-government."

While simple in theory, these objectives would embroil the US into a divisive eight-year conflict.

When Operation Iraqi Freedom (OIF) commenced, it happened sooner than anyone in the CAOC had expected. In fact, for the F-15E crews, there was some lingering confusion as to when Operation Southern Watch ended and when Iraqi Freedom began. Indeed, a flight of four F-15Es was already airborne on a Southern Watch mission when the so-called "Second Gulf War" began. These four Strike Eagles had flown a GBU-28 mission over the Intercept Operations Center at Iraq's H-3 airfield on March 19, 2003. Minutes later, two F-117 Nighthawks departed northward on a strike mission against a house that was purportedly holding Saddam Hussein.

As the F-15Es returned from their H3 strike mission, they were still unaware that Operation Iraqi Freedom has commenced. As they egressed from Iraqi airspace, however, "their radios came alive and blocks of airspace were cleared by AWACS for incoming Tomahawk cruise missiles."

The campaign of "Shock and Awe" had begun.

In the days leading up to OIF, however, a Special Forces task force known as "Task Force Tawny" (TF-20) was conducting a top-secret mission within Iraq. Despite the

US forces uncover an Iraqi MiG-25 buried underneath the sands of Al-Taqqadum Air Base—July 2003. In the days leading up to Operation Iraqi Freedom, the Iraqi Air Force buried and hid many of their fighter jets rather than risk losing them to American F-15s and F-16s. As a result, the air superiority F-15C Eagles had little to do in the skies over Iraq during the Second Gulf War. (US Air Force)

clandestine nature of the operation, however, the Strike Eagles of the 335th Fighter Squadron rendered close air support to the TF-20 commandos. While maintaining their flight patterns over the "kill box"—the designated airspace for the operation—the F-15E pilots would maintain comms with the Special Forces troops via a secure KY-58 radio. To help maintain situational awareness, the SF troops used infrared strobes to communicate their locations to the Strike Eagles—which the pilots could see via their onboard night-vision devices. For the commandos on the ground, their duties ranged from destroying tactical missile sites to killing Baathist leaders. During these operations, the Strike Eagle pilots, or their WSOs, would acquire targets via input from the ground commanders.

On one occasion, a team of SF operators came under fire by a group of Fedayeen militia traveling in a Toyota pickup. Calling on the nearest Strike Eagle, the ground commander asked for close air support against the offending Toyota. The CAOC had ordered them not to fly under 10,000 feet unless there was imminent danger to ground troops. Although it could be argued that these truck-mounted Fedayeen militiamen were hardly an "imminent threat," the lingering F-15Es gladly responded with a burst from their M61A1 guns.

From time to time, SF troops also requested the Strike Eagles to conduct a "show of strength" fly-by at 300 feet, usually at nightfall and directly over where the enemy was known to be hiding. During these fly-bys, the Strike Eagles would drop flares, prompting the enemy to come out of hiding and into the SF team's line of fire.

During these SF-support missions, the embedded air controllers had direct lines of contact to the CAOC and the local AWACS. Because the SF troops were on the ground, with real-time situational awareness, many F-15Es were diverted from their original flight plans to assist troops in contact, or otherwise destroy TSTs. During one such exchange, the AWACS vectored two F-15Es to destroy a pair of Scud launchers hidden in a culvert under Highway 80—the main thoroughfare into Baghdad.

During the first day of the war, both the 335th and 336th made extensive use of the AGM-130 missile against Iraqi targets. Strike Eagles from the 336th, for example, employed the AGM during their attack on the Republican Guard barracks near Baghdad International Airport. The 335th, meanwhile, leveled Saddam's Yacht Club. The F-15Es also flew Offensive Counter Air (OCA) missions that day. While American ground forces began their 80-mile blitzkrieg into Baghdad, the Strike Eagles pushed forward to neutralize any resistance from the Iraqi Air Force. By this time, however, much of Iraq's ailing air force was being destroyed on the ground. There was, however, plenty of anti-aircraft fire during the opening days of the war. As one F-15E pilot recalled, there were at least 40 Iraqi SAM launches during the first hour of the war.

While aloft on their SCAR missions, the 335th and 336th destroyed several Iraqi planes before they could get airborne. By 2003, the Iraqi Air Force was a shadow of what it had been in 1990. What little aircraft remained after Desert Storm were often unserviceable or flown by pilots whose skills had steadily eroded. Thus, it would not take long for any coalition aircraft to make short order of Saddam's withering air fleet. According to the official tally, F-15Es from the 336th Fighter Squadron demolished more than sixty-five MIG-21s, SU-22s, SU-25s, and MIG-23s on the runways, while scouring the terrain for relay stations and air defense sites. The 335th Fighter Squadron,

A Strike Eagle from the 494th Fighter Squadron on a combat sortie in support of Operation Iraqi Freedom on April 22, 2004. As part of its mission package, this F-15E is carrying two AIM-120s, two AIM-9 Sidewinders, four GBU-12s, and a centerline-mounted JDAM bomb. (US Air Force)

meanwhile, achieved more aircraft kills by way of their GBU-12 bombs—all of which was captured on film by their onboard cameras.

For every sortie, the Air Force typically had three AWACS on station—relaying critical communication from the CAOC, directing numerous air assets, and monitoring the ever-changing enemy situation. The AWACS would send directives to the F-15 flight leaders, who in turn would contact the local strike aircraft (typically F-16CJs, F/A-18s, and/or EA-6Bs) regarding the mission directives. During this time, the F-15Es were the vanguards of what the Air Force called "Suppression of Enemy Air Defense" (SEAD) missions. With the F-15Es escorting the F-16CJs and other SEAD assets, the strike airplanes roamed Iraqi airspace, designating targets of interest. Under these auspices, the Strike Eagles aided in the destruction of several Iraqi air defense sites.

Throughout the conflict, whether performing CAS, OCA, or delivering their AGM-130s to any variety of ground targets, the F-15E Strike Eagle's performance was without equal. The 336th Fighter Squadron, for example, logged nearly 6,000 flight hours throughout the conflict—nearly 4,800 of which were combat hours. The Strike Eagle itself finished the Iraq War with a Mission Capable rate of 84.1%—a record bested only by the F-117 Nighthawk, a plane that was, by comparison, far less active throughout the war.

Over the course of Iraqi Freedom, the US lost only one Strike Eagle—the victim of a crash near Tikrit. The exact cause of the crash was never determined, but there remains little doubt that the F-15E Strike Eagle was the workhorse in the skies over Iraq.

While the F-15E Strike Eagle excelled and exerted itself during the Iraq War, its air-

F-15E Strike Eagles taxi down the runway at Balad Air Base, Iraq, after returning from a mission on June 12, 2006.

superiority cousin, the F-15C/D, struggled to find a meaningful mission. Since the Iraqi Air Force was all but destroyed, the "light gray" Eagles had little to do in terms of air combat. The 58th Fighter Squadron, who had distinguished themselves as "MiG Killers" during Desert Storm, deployed to King Faisal Air Base on March 6, 2003. At nearly the same time, the 94th Fighter Squadron deployed to Incirlik Air Base in Turkey, while the 71st Fighter Squadron arrived in Tabuk, Saudi Arabia. Unfortunately, for all three squadrons, there was virtually nothing to engage in the skies over Iraq.

Arriving in theater, the F-15C pilots discovered that their missions would be remarkably similar to the ones they had flown during the days of Operation Northern Watch and Southern Watch. Combat Air Patrols and aerial reconnaissance were, once again, the rule of the day. Between these missions, the pilots conducted a number of training exercises to maintain their tactical edge. To combat the monotony of these cyclic air patrols, some F-15 squadrons partnered with other units to cross-train for different types of aerial missions—CAS and air interdiction, for example. However, the landscape for mission planning was tenuous and extremely fluid. Therefore, these training scenarios did not always come together as planned. Adding to the problem was the ever-tenuous relationship with Turkey and Saudi Arabia—two countries whose regulations for airspace usage seemed to change with the tides.

During the OIF missions, the F-15s flew "on station"—meaning that the pilots were flying over enemy territory in CAP formation, ready to execute any on-call taskings. Typically, these F-15s flew in teams of two to four. Most of the F-15C pilots preferred the two-plane configuration, as they felt that using smaller formations helped them avoid detection and provided them better flexibility to cover the vast territories that they were expected to patrol.

In all, however, OIF was largely uneventful for the "light gray" air superiority F-15Cs. By the start of the conflict, the Iraqi Air Force hardly went aloft, and after Baghdad fell in April 2003, there were no Iraqi aircraft to be found. With virtually no mission to perform, the F-15C squadrons returned home in May 2003. It was said that they were simply wasting fuel and "burning holes in the sky."

OIF was, nevertheless, a veritable proving ground for the F-15E Strike Eagle. In many respects, the Iraq War may have been the Strike Eagle's finest endeavor. The intrepid pilots and WSOs were mentally prepared for whatever the mission required of them. Among its many accomplishments, the F-15E was credited with killing more than sixty-five Iraqi aircraft while they were still on the ground.

The Iraq War continued over the ensuing decade until, in August 2010, President Barack Obama proclaimed an end to combat operations. Operation Iraqi Freedom thus became "Operation New Dawn"—a yearlong advisory mission wherein a provisional number of U.S. troops remained in Iraq to assist and advise the post-Saddam forces. On December 18, 2011, the last American forces left Iraq—marking the official end to what had been a bloody seven-year conflict that claimed the lives of nearly 4,500 American servicemen. Little did anyone realize, however, that within a few years, American forces would return to Iraq to fight a new enemy—a fundamentalist organization known as the Islamic State of Iraq and Syria (ISIS).

Eagle Sunset

In February 2011, as part of what the international media had dubbed the "Arab Spring," the State of Libya erupted in civil war. Under the leadership of Muammar al-Gaddafi, Libya had had a long and tumultuous relationship with the United States. The first conflict with Gaddafi erupted over his so-called "Line of Death"— a term by which he declared the entire Gulf of Sidra as Libyan territorial water. Twice, in 1981 and 1989, Libyan planes had engaged American F-14s over the Gulf of Sidra. In both instances, the F-14s made short work of the offending aircraft.

This F-15E from the 492d Fighter Squadron, piloted by US Air Force Major Lucas Teel and his WSO Lieutenant Clint Mixon, prepares to depart RAF Lakenheath on March 19, 2011. Its destination is Libya, where it will be initiating precision air strikes in support of Operation Odyssey Dawn, the military campaign against the forces of Muammar Al-Gaddafi. (US Air Force)

The Strike Eagle numbered "91-0304/LN," which crashed in Libya on March 22, 2011 while flying a combat mission in support of Operation Odyssey Dawn. The pilot and WSO safely ejected and were later rescued. (KGYST)

From his support of terrorist groups, to his attempts at nuclear power, and his insistence on the nautical "Line of Death," US-Libyan tensions peaked on April 5, 1986, when Gaddafi's agents orchestrated the bombing of a night club in West Berlin. Three people were killed, including a US serviceman; 299 were injured— 63 of whom were American.

Almost simultaneously, the Reagan Administration began researching potential targets for a strike on Libya. The goal was to decimate Gaddafi's terrorist infrastructure, disrupt his internal operations, and deplete his military resources. All told, President Reagan saw the West Berlin nightclub as a direct attack on the United States. "Self-defense is not only our right," he said, "it is our duty." Invoking international law, Reagan said: "It is the purpose behind the mission...a mission fully consistent with Article 51 of the UN Charter." Thus, on April 14, 1986, the US launched Operation El Dorado Canyon, an inter-service airstrike that left a devastating impact on Tripoli and Benghazi.

By the mid-1990s, however, Gaddafi had dialed down his rhetoric and had made diplomatic strides to "mend fences" with the international community. Still, to the US, he was no trustworthy ally. Thus, it came as little surprise when, on March 19, 2011 (exactly eight years from the start of the Second Gulf War), the US and NATO led a military intervention in support of anti-Gaddafi forces. Under the codename "Operation Odyssey Dawn," the US led a multi-faceted air campaign against the ailing forces of Muammar al-Gaddafi.

As part of the recurring air campaign, ten F-15E Strike Eagles from the 492d and 494th Fighter Squadrons struck air defense targets before shifting their focus to mobile TSTs. On March 22, 2011, the fourth day of the air campaign, an F-15E from the 492d Fighter Squadron crashed in Libya after suffering an onboard mechanical failure. Landing about 25 miles southwest of Benghazi, the pilot and WSO successfully ejected from the Strike Eagle, but were soon separated amidst the confusion of the bailout.

Marines assigned to the 26th Marine Expeditionary Unit conduct electronic checks on their CH–53E Super Stallion Helicopters before taking off to rescue the downed crew of the F-15E Strike Eagle "91-0304/LN." (US Navy)

When coalition air commanders received the distress call from the downed F-15E, they soon launched a rescue mission to retrieve the downed aviators. Calling on the 26th Marine Expeditionary Unit, a MV-22 Osprey helicopter and two AV-8B Harrier jets were dispatched to recover the downed aircrew. The Ospreys arrived overhead at 2:19 AM, confirming contact with the downed pilot, who was safely onboard the rescue helicopter by 3:00 AM. The wayward WSO, however, was rescued by Libyan rebels and quickly shuttled to a 'safe house,' where he was later recovered by US forces.

At one point during the rescue operation, the downed pilot called upon two Harriers to drop their 500-pound bombs near his location; apparently there was a group of unidentified persons heading his way, and he wanted the bombs dropped as a "terrain-denial maneuver." Later that night, US forces bombed the wreckage of the F-15E to prevent its onboard avionics from "falling into the wrong hands."

Airstrikes continued for the next 161 days, ending with the capture of Muammar al-Gaddafi on October 20, 2011.

Operation Inherent Resolve

Since the rise of The Islamic State of Iraq and Syria (ISIS), the F-15E Strike Eagle and A-10 Thunderbolt (commonly known as the "Warthog") have been the primary workhorses in the air campaign against Islamic terrorists in the Middle East.

ISIS and its followers were strict adherents to Sharia Law— a code of conduct based on literal interpretations of the Koran and Islamic theology. Taking advantage of the post-war instability in Iraq (and the frailty of the new Iraqi Army), ISIS operatives quickly overran Tikrit, Mosul, Raqqa, and Fallujah in 2014—declaring those cities as part of their new "caliphate." Because Mosul was a city of more than two million people, its calamitous fall to the hands of ISIS took the world by surprise. ISIS leader Abu Bakr al-Baghdadi then appointed himself "caliph" of the newly conquered territories.

In one of his first official acts as "caliph," Al-Baghdadi promised that anyone who defied his authority would be summarily stoned or publicly beheaded. Following this proclamation, thousands were killed as ISIS tightened its grip on Iraq. Many surviving women were forced into slavery. That summer, ISIS beheaded two American journalists— James Foley and Steven Sotloff— and broadcast the decapitations on YouTube. These barbarous acts drew fierce condemnation from the international community, but condemnation alone would not stop ISIS.

Refusing to stand by and let Iraq fall to the wrath of the Islamic State, the US and its allies launched Operation Inherent Resolve— a combined effort to destroy the Islamic State within the borders of Iraq and Syria. With multi-national forces working in concert to destroy the ISIS footholds and break their occupation, Allied drones and fighter-bombers have thus far dropped more than 67,000 pieces of ordnance since 2014.

During the battles to reconquer Iraq's northern cities, American F-15Es and A-10s flew into the densely-populated urban areas to gather intelligence and engage ground targets. In the early days of Operation Inherent Resolve, one squadron commander likened these airstrikes to the bombing campaigns of World War II— adding that his pilots "had to get

An F-15E Strike Eagle flies over northern Iraq early on the morning of September 23, 2014, after conducting airstrikes against ISIS targets in Syria. Under the banner of Operation Inherent Resolve, this F-15E was a part of the inaugural strike force to engage targets against the Islamic State. (US Air Force)

At Incirlik Air Base, Turkey, an F–15E Strike Eagle sits on the tarmac shortly after returning from another bombing mission over Syria on November 12, 2015. (US Air Force)

creative to figure out ways to strike targets at the bottom of these five story buildings."

On the morning of September 23, 2014, numerous coalition aircraft (including the F–15E Strike Eagle) conducted air strikes in Syria against several Islamic State targets. These included training compounds, command and control facilities, caches, personnel and vehicles. Later that day, the Pentagon released video footage of ISIS targets being destroyed by American F–15Es. What made the videos more astonishing was that they'd been taken by the Strike Eagles' own AN/AAQ-33 Sniper targeting pods. A highly-sophisticated camera and surveillance system designed by Lockheed Martin, the AN/AAQ-33 was officially termed the "Sniper Advanced Targeting Pod." The pod itself is equipped with a laser designator used to guide precision bombs and also features a Forward Looking Infra-Red (FLIR) system with a CCD-TV camera. The optics are used for identifying air and ground targets, tracking, and navigational coordinate generation.

During these opening months of Inherent Resolve, F–15E Strike Eagles conducted thirty-seven percent of all US Air Force sorties over Iraq and Syria. Soon, however, the fighting spread to Libya. In the wake of Muammar al-Gaddafi's downfall, Libya had plunged into chaos— allowing ISIS leaders to partially fill the vacuum in the wake of that dictator's demise. Throughout the late summer and fall of 2015, American F–15Es flying from RAF Lakenheath in the United Kingdom flew several long-range bombing missions against targets in Libya. On November 13, 2015, for example, a pair of F–15Es killed Abu Nabil-Anbari, the purported leader of ISIS in Libya.

In February 2016, a flight of F–15E Strike Eagles destroyed an Islamic State training camp near Sabratha, Libya. Among the camp's occupants were Noureddine Chouchane,

An F-15E sits in its revetment during a break in operations supporting Inherent Resolve, 2017. (US Air Force)

a 36-year-old ISIS operative who had been linked to the Sousse attacks of 2015. Sources indicated that 49 people were killed during the F-15E air strike— including two Serbian nationals whom had been kidnapped by ISIS months earlier.

While these F-15Es took flight, their partnering KC-135 aero-tankers flew 12-13 sorties every day to keep the aircraft fueled. The refuel missions ran in six-hour shifts. As one Air Force officer recalled: "For a lot of our young crews that come out here, it's the first time that they've seen, when they cross from Turkish airspace into the combat zone, how often the plan changes; the locations that they're refueling, amounts of off-load, times, where they have to be. And it can be a little overwhelming for them…but they pick it up pretty quick, and by the time they've flown a sortie or two, it's second nature."

By the end of 2016, superior airpower and coalition ground offenses had largely beaten back the ISIS juggernaut. With AWACS and Strike Eagles in the air, coalition ground commanders were never at a loss for proper air support. When ground maneuvers had finally shoe-horned ISIS into narrower confines, coalition FACs called in air strikes with deadly accuracy. CENTCOM's Air Component Commander, Lieutenant General Jeffrey Harrigian, later recalled: "When suicide vehicle bombers raced toward exposed [Iraqis], airpower delivered precision weapons to stop the enemy forces from completing their grisly mission." When commenting on the pinpoint accuracy of the F-15E Strike Eagle and other attack aircraft in theater, Harrigian added: "We have refined our targeting process and become more efficient in layering our ISR to uncover targets that have made themselves available to us, which also has facilitated the number of weapons we've been able to deliver."

Such was the case on June 8, 2017, when an F-15E Strike Eagle shot down a Syrian drone near the city of Al Tanf. According to US officials, the Syrian drone was shot down after it deployed "one of several weapons it was carrying near a position occupied by Coalition personnel." According to the US military, the Syrian drone was likely an Iranian-built Shahed 129 UCAV. Twelve days later, on June 20, 2017, an F-15E shot down a confirmed Shahed-129 near the 50-mile exclusion zone surrounding Al-Tanf. In both instances, the Strike Eagles were able to deliver their ordnance with pinpoint accuracy, from stand-off distances, and with minimal collateral damage.

In the ongoing campaigns against ISIS, American F-15Es have delivered thousands of pounds of ordnance and logged several hundred flight hours of reconnaissance and intelligence gathering. According to CENTCOM, the F-15E Strike Eagle and A-10 Warthog have collectively dropped nearly 15,000 pieces of ordnance on ISIS targets since the beginning of Inherent Resolve.

At this writing, ISIS has lost nearly 98 percent of the territory it acquired in 2014–15. The Allied air and ground campaigns have diminished the Islamic State to a fraction of its former size and capabilities. Although ISIS is no longer considered the imminent threat it once was, the venomous organization still operates on a degraded scale and, at this writing, the US-led coalition is still engaged in Operation Inherent Resolve.

The Yemeni Insurgency

In 2015, as the Republic of Yemen devolved further into civil war— pitting the insurgent Houthi faction against the loyalist Hadi movement— Saudi Arabia led an intervention into Yemen to stem the tide of sectarian violence. King Salman of Saudi Arabia declared that Saudi air and ground forces would spearhead the effort to restore the Hadi regime. The United Nations, meanwhile, sanctioned the Houthi rebels with an arms embargo.

The first wave of Saudi-led airstrikes began on March 26, 2015— under the codename "Operation Decisive Storm." Leading the Royal Saudi Air Force (RSAF) into battle were their own versions of the F-15E Strike Eagle: the specially-modified "F-15S" fighters. The F-15S was exported to Saudi Arabia during the 1990s. As an export variant, the only difference between the F-15S and its F-15E counterpart is the AN/APG-70's radar performance. More than 70 F-15S airframes were delivered to the RSAF.

As the Saudi F-15s began striking targets in Yemen, they were countered initially by piecemeal anti-aircraft fire from pro-Houthi forces. These early F-15 strikes were aimed at air defense sites, missile depots, launchers and other critical targets. During these opening attacks, however, a Saudi F-15S crashed into the Gulf of Aden while circling over the sea. The two pilots ejected and were later recovered from the sea by a US Air Force HH-60G rescue helicopter.

Throughout the Saudi-led intervention, US air squadrons provided aero-tanker support, and rescued downed aviators. Reviewing the crash, Saudi authorities concluded that the F-15S had crashed due to engine failure. Houthi and Iranian sources, however, claimed they had shot down the F-15.

On January 8, 2018, another Saudi F-15S was reportedly shot down by a Houthi SAM. Houthi operatives then released a video showing the Saudi F-15 conducting evasive maneuvers and deploying flares. The video footage showed the F-15S being struck by

An F-15 Eagle flies along an F-22 Raptor, the plane that will eventually replace the former. The F-22 is considered the first of the "fifth-generation" fighters, incorporating advanced avionics and stealth technology (US Air Force).

something, but it was unclear if it was the SAM as indicated by Houthi forces. Whatever the projectile had been, it had obviously done damage to the plane, but not to the extent that would cause the plane to crash. Indeed, the following day, January 9, the Houthi media confirmed that the F-15 had been damaged but did not crash.

On March 21, 2018, Houthi operatives released another video purportedly showing a Saudi F-15 being hit by a R-27 air-to-air missile that had been adapted for surface-to-air use. As with the previous video of January 8, this F-15S had clearly been hit, but it did not fall from the sky. Later, the RSAF confirmed that the F-15 had been hit, but later landed safely at a Saudi airbase.

The RSAF was the only coalition participant to use an F-15 variant during the fight against Yemeni insurgents. As the war progressed, however, the aerial campaign shifted its focus from using strike-fighters to using drones. To this end, the coalition partners acquired a number of Chinese-made drones, along with a cadre of Russian fighter planes to assist in the ongoing War with Yemen. Indeed, while the appearance of an F-15S may not be as prevalent as it was during the early months of the campaign, the Arabian Eagle remains a viable asset in the fight against Yemeni insurgents.

The Future of the F-15

There has been a silent understanding that most fighter jets have a lifespan of approximately 30 years. As of 2019, the US Air Force is using the oldest fleet of aircraft in its operational history. Indeed, vaunted fighters like the F-15 Eagle and F-16 Fighting Falcon are now well beyond the 40-year mark. The new F-22 Raptor and F-35 Lighting, however, have provided American fighter squadrons with a new tactical and technological edge. As the US military returns its focus to preparing for conventional, force-on-force conflicts, the time is right to reinvest in its tactical air superiority.

According to Air Force General James "Mike" Holmes, the commander-in-chief of Air Combat Command, there are "smart, tough, capable peer adversaries [who] have watched us since the 1990s, and they took notes." These latter-day adversaries include Russia, Iran, China, and North Korea among others. Many of these potential adversaries have developed their own "smart" weapons with capabilities comparable to the US. General Holmes added that: "The US simply can't posture itself and operate in ways it has gotten used to or there will be ugly surprises ahead." The implication, therefore, is that America's next conflict will bear no resemblance to those it fought when the F-15 was on the cutting edge of technology.

In a 2007 interview, Air Force Chief of Staff, General Michael Mosley said: "The F-15s and F-16s were designed and built in the late '60s and '70s. Some of them were produced up until the early '80s. They have fought valiantly for seventeen years of straight combat [referring to Desert Storm, Northern/Southern Watch, the Balkans, and the Global War on Terror]. These planes must be replaced because they have been continually restricted in terms of speed and maneuverability. It was designed to be a Mach 2.5 airplane. Maneuverability is another problem because we've had tail cracks, fuselage cracks, cracks in the wings."

Secretary of the Air Force Michael Wynne used the following analogy: "It's almost like going to the Indy 500 race practicing all the way up until Memorial Day at 60 miles

A Japanese F-15 in flight. Manufactured under contract by Mitsubishi Industries, the Japanese Air Self-Defense Force remains one of the primary foreign operators of the F-15 Eagle. However, in recent years, the Japanese government has considered selling their fleet of F-15s in favor of the new F-35 Lightning. (US Air Force)

an hour, and then on game day, accelerating the car out to 200 miles an hour. It's not the time to be doing that on game day. So, in our training models and in our scenarios, we're limiting these airplanes because they're restricted and getting old. So, there's two parts to the recapitalization of the fighter inventory. The first part is the existing stuff is old and it's getting broke, and it's getting harder to get it out of depot on time. And our availability rates and our in-commission rates are going down. The ability to generate the sorties on those old airplanes is in the wrong direction." Meanwhile, CENTCOM's Air Component Commander, Lieutenant General Gary North, remarked that his fleet of newer-model F-15s are fully mission capable, but added that: "I worry about the health of our aging fleet."

Taking these points into consideration, it comes as no surprise that the F-15 Eagle will likely be phased out of service within the next twenty years. Indeed, it seems that the F-22 Raptor and F-35 Lightning will become the new mainstays of American fighter squadrons for well into the 21st Century. That being said, the immediate fate of the F-15 Eagle and F-15 Strike Eagle remains uncertain.

It is likely, however, that several F-15s will remain in service with the Air National Guard for long after they have been withdrawn from the active duty fleet. Eventually, these National Guard "hand-me-downs" may be sold to allied nations or permanently retired to the infamous "Boneyard" at Davis-Monthan Air Force Base.

Although the F-15 is approaching the twilight of its career, it remains a viable airframe for the United States and several allied air forces. Israel, for example, has owned the F-15 since the late 1970s. To this day, the "Baz" and "Ra'am" variants remain a source of national pride. More recently, the Israeli Air Force acquired the latest version of the F-15D, updated with "fast pack" fuel tanks, giving it greater endurance for aerial reconnaissance and long-range airstrikes.

The 173d Fighter Wing of the US Air National Guard thus donated nine F-15Ds to Israel in September 2016. Although these planes may have been "aging" by American standards, the Israeli Air Force regarded them as an unparalleled investment in maintaining air superiority. In an official statement, the Israeli Air Force said of the F-15Ds: "The aircraft were decommissioned by the USANG as a part of a natural decommissioning process, and were supposed to be used for spare parts. However, the service members of the IAF's Materiel Directorate and Technical Branch recognized their potential: two-seat F-15 fighter jets with the ability to carry Conformal Fuel Tanks (CFT)."

In a similar vein, the Qatari Air Force negotiated a $12 billion contract with Boeing in 2017 to purchase thirty-six F-15 fighters, modified according to Qatari specifications. The Qatari government may purchase as many as 72 additional F-15s by 2022. Meanwhile, the Japanese Air Self-Defense Force continues to fly its own version of Eagle— the F-15J, developed under contract by Mitsubishi Industries. In 2018, however, the Japanese Ministry of Defense announced that they are considering selling their F-15Js in favor of the new F-35. Meanwhile, the Korean Air Force proudly maintains the F-15K "Slam Eagle"— their own derivative of the F-15E. South Korea plans to keep the strike fighter in service beyond the year 2055.

At this writing, there are several upgrades pending for the current fleet of American F-15s.

An F-15C Eagle from the 144th Fighter Wing, California Air National Guard, flies high over the Canadian tundra during Exercise Vigilant Shield, 2015. Although the F-15 Eagle and Strike Eagle are in the "twilight" of their collective service life, the US Air Force plans to keep the fighter within its frontline inventory for the next several years. As the F-22 Raptor and F-35 Lightning replace the F-15 Eagle in the active duty force, the latter will likely continue in service with the Air National Guard for many years thereafter. (US Air Force)

For example, the APG-70 radar aboard the Strike Eagle is being replaced by the APG-82 AESA. Improved avionics and communication modules will also be featured aboard the enhanced F-15s. Updated landing gear will allow the Eagles and Strike Eagles to perform 1,400 takeoffs and landings before necessitating wheel and brake replacements. Armaments and onboard tracking systems will likewise be updated. For example, with the Advanced Missile Bomb Ejector Rack, the F-15's missile haulage will increase to 22 ordnances per mission— a significant increase from their previous capacity of 16.

Synchronicity of communication remains a recurring issue in the quest to maintain air superiority— and the F-15 Eagle is no exception. As the US military continues the trend of digitizing its combat communications (instead of relying on radio transmissions), the Air Force has made strides to adopt a common digital communication platform for all its aircraft. Under this system, an F-15 could, theoretically, share real-time digital reports with the other planes in its squadron, or even a nearby A-10 or B-52. Currently, the US Air Force and Boeing Aerospace are running tests between the F-22 Raptor and the F-15C to determine the best methods of data synchronicity. According to Lieutenant General Jerry D. Harris Jr., the Air Force Deputy Chief of Staff for Strategic Plans and Requirements: "These experiments are demonstrating correlation/fusion of data from multiple sources, including intelligence sources, fourth and fifth generation fighters."

This need for a real-time, multi-tiered communication system precipitated development of the Advanced Display Core Processor II— the "world's fastest military aircraft mission computer," as Boeing calls it. Complementing this upgrade is the Eagle Passive/Active Warning Survivability System— described as "the most powerful electronic warfare suite" by its developer, BAE Systems. As of 2019, Boeing has already mounted the new Raytheon APG-63(V)3 AESA radar onto 125 of the approximately 200 F-15C Eagles slated to receive this upgrade. Boeing is also preparing to install the Raytheon APG-82 radar into nearly 200 F-15E Strike Eagles.

Conceived as a counterbalance to the MiG-25, the F-15 Eagle began its journey into history during the twilight of the Vietnam War. As a boon to reclaim American air superiority, the F-15 has dominated the skies in combats large and small. Whether fulfilling the role of an aerial dogfighter, interceptor, or ground-attack aircraft, the F-15 has proven its worth in the service of air forces worldwide. Throughout its service life, the F-15 has undergone several upgrades to its airframe, avionics, armament, and powertrain. Today, nearly 700 F-15 variants remain in active service with the US Air Force. As Steven Parker, former Vice President of Boeing's F-15 operations, once said: "For an in-production air superiority aircraft, nothing compares to an F-15 today. Nothing flies faster; nothing goes higher; nothing carries more."

As the F-15 now lumbers into its *fifth* decade of service, it remains a highly-adaptive, multi-role, air superiority fighter…undefeated in aerial combat.

Select Bibliography

Aloni, Shlomo. *Israeli F-15 Eagle Units in Combat*. London: Bloomsbury Publishing, 2013.

Brown, Craig. *Debrief: A Complete History of U.S. Aerial Engagements 1981 to the Present*. Atglen: Schiffer Pub, 2007.

Davies, Steve. *Boeing F-15E Strike Eagle: All Weather Attack Aircraft*. Crowood Press, 2003.

Davies, Steve. F-15C *Eagle Units in Combat*. Oxford: Osprey Publishing, 2005.

Davies, Steve. F-15E *Strike Eagle Units in Combat 1990–2005*. Oxford: Osprey Publishing, 2005.

Davies, Steve. *McDonnell Douglas/Boeing F-15 Eagle Manual: 1972 onwards (all marks)*. Haynes Publishing UK, 2014.

Davies, Steve, and Doug Dildy. *F-15 Eagle Engaged: The world's most successful jet fighter*. Oxford: Osprey Publishing, 2007.

Drendel, Lou, and Don Greer. *F-15 Eagle*. 2001.

Hallion, Richard. *Storm Over Iraq: Air Power and the Gulf War*. New York: Smithsonian Institution, 2015.

Lambeth, Benjamin S. *NATO's Air War for Kosovo: A Strategic and Operational Assessment*. Santa Monica: Rand Corporation, 2001.

Morse, Stan. *Gulf Air War: Debrief*. Airtime Pub, 1991.

McCarthy, Donald J. *The Raptors: All F-15 and F-16 Aerial Combat Victories*. Altgen: Schiffer Pub, 2017.

Ripley, Tim. *Air War Afghanistan: US and NATO Air Operations from 2001*. Pen & Sword, 2011.

United States Air Force. *McDonnell Douglas F-15E Strike Eagle Pilot's Flight Operating Instructions*. Washington, DC: US Government Printing Office, 2010.

United States Air Force. *The F-15 Eagle: Origins and Development 1964-1972*. Washington DC: Government Printing Office, 2019.